Copyright © 2022 Matthew Douglas Pinard

All Rights Reserved. No part of this book publication may be reproduced or transmitted in any form or by any means, mechanical or electronic, including photocopying, scanning, and recording, or by any information storage and retrieval system, or other -- without prior permission in writing from the author or publisher. Disclaimers: The Publisher and the Author make no representation or warranties concerning the accuracy or completeness of the contents of this work and specifically disclaim all warranties for a particular purpose. No warranty may be created or extended through sales or promotional materials. The advice and strategies contained herein may not be suitable for every situation. This work is sold with the understanding that the Author and Publisher are not engaged in rendering legal, technological, or other professional services. If professional assistance is required, the services of a competent professional should be sought. Neither the Publisher nor the Author shall be liable for damages arising therefrom. The fact that an organization or website is referred to in this work as a citation and/or potential source of further information does not mean that the Author or the Publisher endorses the information, the organization, or website it may provide, or recommendations it may make. Further, readers should be aware that the websites listed in this work may have changed or disappeared between the time that this work was written and when it is read. Details of the cases and stories in this book have been changed to preserve privacy.

Printed in the United States of America
Published by: Writer's Publishing House
Prescott, Az 86301

Cover and Interior Design by Creative Artistic Excellence Marketing
Project Management and Book Launch by Creative Artistic Excellence Marketing
https://lizzymcnett.com

Paperback ISBN: 978-1-64873-264-5
Hardcover ISBN: 978-1-64873-265-2
Ebook ISBN: 978-1-64873-266-9

Table of Contents

Paxton Elkins — 5

Shaman's Blues — 25

Blinded by the Light — 33

Lord of Hosts — 39

Ghost Light — 44

Stark Hypnotherapy — 51

Nibiru System — 61

Green Eyed Lady — 64

Buffalo — 93

Universal Mind — 106

Yes, the River Knows — 109

The Crystal Ship — 111

The Soft Parade — 113

L.A. Woman — 121

The End — 126

Peace Town — 144

Purple and Free — 146

Other Books by Author Matthew — 149

Screenplay Awards — 152

Matthew Douglas Pinard — 153

The New Wine
Volume II

Peace Town

Paxton Elkins

Photo: Mr. Paxton Elkins wearing his "Paxton's Army" gear. This is both his mother and I's favorite photo of him. His long eyelashes are simply beautiful. There is no question in my mind that he is an incarnate son of St. Mary.

On Sunday, October 15th, 2017 at 7:25 a.m., young Paxton Elkins, aged eight, who was initially introduced in the first volume of The New Wine, died peacefully at his home in Portage, Indiana, surrounded by his loving family. I recall waking up that morning feeling "off" the entire day. I knew something was different. It was not until later in the evening that I heard from his family that he had gone to be with St. Mary that morning. I am dedicating this entire book to the memory of his remarkable life. Paxton's life, although very short, was extremely meaningful nonetheless. He lived fifteen months after he was diagnosed with diffuse intrinsic pontine glioma or DIPG. Only 3 percent of children diagnosed with DIPG live past nine months. I believe we were granted an extra six months with him by God the Father.

There is no doubt in my mind that Paxton was an incarnate son of St. Mary. As stated in the first volume of The New Wine, Paxton translates to "peace town" which is also the subtitle of the second volume of The New Wine. In fact, Paxton and I comprise what Jim Morrison and I sang in "Waiting for the Sun" as referenced in the line "it's time to live in the scattered sun." What's interesting is Paxton and his brother Landon were both conceived right around the same time my wife and I had two miscarriages. He and I are the "scattered sons" of St. Mary. Paxton, Jim

Morrison, and myself also comprise part of a Bible prophecy/passage that Jesus gave thousands of years ago. The passage states, "How many times are you supposed to forgive your brother? seventy times seven," Jesus stated. If you take Paxton's age of seven when I first met him and the combined ages of Jim and myself being seventy years old when we first met, you have seventy times seven. I do not believe this is a coincidence. Why do I believe this all to be true? The day after Paxton died on Monday, October 16th, 2017, at exactly 3 p.m. at the exact moment I was thinking of the last hug I received from him that he gave me for praying to "take his pain for him," my silver Christian cross bent nearly in half,

    The Sunday afternoon that Paxton passed away, another "half rainbow" (like the two fraternal twin rainbows that appeared in the skies of West Michigan that initially led me to Paxton and his family) appeared again almost in the exact same location as the first half fraternal twin rainbow that appeared a year earlier. The half rainbow to me was a sign for Paxton's life. His life was not fulfilled completely and not yet a "full rainbow" at the time of his DIPG cancer diagnosis and tragic passing. Earlier in the summer, we had a second very interesting looking full rainbow appear just like the first one that went across the skies as shown in the first volume of The New Wine.

Photo: This incredible image shows my Christian cross missing the body of Christ that fell off of it as it also bent nearly in half on its own, the day after young Paxton Elkins passed away.

Photo: This remarkable rainbow appeared in the summer of 2017, prior to Paxton Elkins passing away.

It is remarkably similar to the full rainbow of the first set of "fraternal twin" rainbows that appeared in our skies the Fall of 2016 that led me to the Elkins family originally. This full rainbow appeared shortly after the full lunar/solar eclipse in our skies.

Photo: Another fraternal twin, half rainbow appears in the skies near Muskegon, Michigan, on the afternoon of Sunday, October 15th, 2017, the date of Paxton's passing away from this earth.

The other reason I am quite certain that Paxton is an incarnate son of St. Mary is the manner in which he left this world. After we prayed with him for the last time in front of a statue of St. Mary at St. Paul's Catholic Church in Valparaiso, Indiana, to simply ask for God to "take the pain away," his family stated that he left this world in absolutely no pain whatsoever. In fact, a few days before he passed away, Paxton told many families and friends that he was "going to be with Jesus" and that "Jesus was a blonde man" who told him he could have many toys including My Little Ponies at his "mansion" in heaven. When I heard this, I immediately began to believe that Paxton was most likely being visited by Archangel Gabriel, who I had been praying for via St. Mary to come down to earth to assist us in this difficult time. The day that Paxton was buried on Friday, October 20th, 2017, at his grave site, the following image of two large archangel wings appeared in the sky at the cemetery:

Photo: Two very large angel wings of Archangel Gabriel appeared in the skies above Paxton's burial site in Portage, Indiana, during his funeral services. Paxton was visited by a "blonde man" the week before who told him he was going to have a mansion with Jesus in heaven. Gabriel is a blonde male archangel from the other kingdom.

Illustration: An image of the blonde Archangel Gabriel who is the messenger angel of God who is also the only one authorized to announce the birth and death of Jesus Christ.

Photo: The flyer handed out in memory of young Paxton Elkins at his memorial services on Thursday, October 19th, 2017.

Photo: The incredibly wonderful Mr. Paxton Elkins prior to his untimely passing this past fall of 2017. He's placing his hand up to a painted hand during a treatment for DIPG. We prayed many times together at St. Paul's Catholic Church in Valparaiso, Indiana, for St. Mary to "stop the pain" by similarly placing our palms together. Paxton is wearing his "Paxton's Army" shirt to show he's a fearless soldier in this war against DIPG.

Photo: This very old family photo of myself with my siblings was taken in the early 1980s. I am sitting to the far left in the picture. I think you will see a very stark resemblance to my childhood photo and the one above it of Paxton Elkins around the same age. We were supposed to meet each other on this side. There is no doubt about this in my mind. We are the "scattered son" Jim and I sang of on "Waiting for the Sun."

    I want to now show an incredible photo taken off the beaches of Lake Michigan during the summer of 2017. On a morning I had been praying for St. Mary to either remove Paxton's brain tumor completely or to have the disease transferred into my own brain, a choir of angels appeared in the sky. Now this request might seem impossible to many; however, shortly after meeting the Elkins family, I met a woman at a Catholic church in Elkhart, Indiana. This woman told me that her best friend made a similar request to St. Mary to take the terminal cancer from her husband. The woman died a few days later at exactly 3 p.m. of the cancer that her husband then miraculously recovered from. I was more than happy to return to the other kingdom if my Father allowed me to take this burden from the Elkins family. Soon after reciting such prayers, I received the most amazing image in the skies above Lake Michigan as I swam near the beach in the summer of 2017.

Photo: A beautiful sunny day off the local beaches of Lake Michigan near Ferrysburg, Michigan, in the summer of 2017. This can only be described as what I would explain as a "choir of angels" surrounding and praying to the middle "angel" with its smaller flailing arms. This choir of angels disappeared almost immediately after I took this photo.

Photo: On the same summer afternoon in 2017 that the "choir of angels" appeared above me on the beaches of Lake Michigan, I stopped by to thank my mother St. Mary at St. Mary's Catholic Church in Spring Lake, Michigan, and was given this glimpse of more "angels on high."

Photo: This was a typical sunset all summer long in Grand Haven, Michigan, in 2017 as I prayed daily for the life of Paxton Elkins. This type of sunset happened out in West Michigan almost nightly as the sun often "danced" and "shimmered" before reluctantly setting in the skies over Lake Michigan.

The morning of Paxton Elkins funeral service on Friday, October 20th, 2017, I was praying inside the adoration chapel at St. Paul's Catholic Church in Valparaiso, Indiana. I showed a photo of Paxton to the large, life-sized bronze statue of St. Mary inside the church and asked her if she could show me where his spirit was presently at. I was immediately flooded with a rapid sequence of flashing images showing Jesus Christ on the cross at the hill on Calvary. The hanging lifeless body of Jesus started to lurch forward and broke off the cross and flew up into the air and immediately turned into a large white-winged dove that flew very high into the sky. The dove opened its wings, and thousands of smaller, white winged doves fell out and started falling from the sky. The smaller doves then turned into lit candles and fell onto the white crosses of buried soldiers at Arlington National Cemetery. It was quite an incredible revelation that I was shown by St. Mary. I don't have all the answers all the time in the present moment, and this is because our Father sometimes withholds things even from me for reasons I can't always see in the present.

Illustration: Another incredible piece of artwork by artist Don Williams, showing a white-winged dove dropping lit candles from its wings, the morning of Paxton Elkins funeral. I received this image from St. Mary while praying in the adoration chapel of St. Paul's Catholic Church in Valparaiso, Indiana, after asking St. Mary to show me where Paxton was now at. This image also reminds one of "come on, baby, light my fire" as Jim Morrison used to sing with the musical group The Doors. Paxton helped to light the fires of fallen soldiers in Paxton's Army. Don's amazing artwork can be found at www.donwilliams.daportfolio.com.

I had been struggling with helping Paxton's family to understand why such an amazingly loving and spiritually powerful, young man who perfectly embodied the concept of God's agape love would be taken from us. My understanding from St. Mary is his soul was needed to "light the fires" of the souls of the deceased U.S. soldiers who had given their lives for this country. This fit right in with the motif of Paxton's Army which was started by his family to bring awareness to the condition of DIPG cancer. It also reminds me of a time I used to sing with my fraternal twin, James, the song, "Light My Fire" by The Doors. Last time I checked Jim and I's royalties from the sales of Doors music albums was worth over eighty million dollars. I think today, if I had proper access to those royalties which are as much mine as they are Jim's, would I be able to cure DIPG brain cancer with that amount? It's what I believe this country with our unending supply of vast riches should be doing. After all, we spend annually half a trillion dollars on actual weapons of mass destruction but choose not to take even one tenth of that amount to cure pediatric brain cancer. On the Saturday after Paxton was laid to rest, the following sunset appeared in the skies of West Michigan:

Photo: a glimpse of the other kingdom taken on the Saturday in West Michigan after we finally laid Paxton Elkins to rest. This is now where Paxton Elkins is no doubt sitting on the Father's throne next to St. Mary surrounded by his choir of angels.

It is my sincere belief that this world has not heard the last from young Paxton Elkins. Do I believe he may return to this earth one day? Yes, I sincerely believe that is entirely possible. In fact, I told his family not to be surprised if a kid approaches them years down the road to tell them he thinks he might be their son. I don't know if this will happen or not, but it is possible. As I stated in the first volume of The New Wine, there is no doubt in my mind that I lived a previous life as James Douglas Morrison, only to be reborn three years later as Matthew Douglas Pinard. I think of Jim's lyrics to the song "Love Me Two Times" where he sings, "love me two times, baby, love me twice today, love me two times, girl, I'm going away." Here he's predicting that the world will get to love him twice and that he would be going away for a while after dying in Paris before returning.

Another The Doors song that seems to support my theory on the Jim to Matt reincarnation and the discovery of the other half of the "scattered son" (Paxton) can be found in the lyrics from "Shaman's Blues." At a Catholic mass, we receive the holy sacrament of "communion." Consider for a moment this term. Communion is a derivative of the English word for "communicating." Communion is how I "communicate" with the other kingdom. "Shaman's Blues" is a perfect example of how two fraternal twin sons of St. Mary can "commune" with each other "across linear time." Jim considered himself a "shaman" or healer like an Indian medicine man who could peer into the spirit world and receive communication to be used as a spiritual guide for the world.

Shaman's Blues

There will never be another one like you

There will never be another one who can do the things you do

Will you give another chance?

Will you try, little try?

Please stop and you remember, we were together,

Anyway, all right

And if you have a certain evening you could lend to me

I'd give it all right back to you and how it has to be

I know your moves, and your mind, and your mind

Will you stop and think and wonder

Just what you'll see, out on the train yard

Nursin' penitentiary, it's gone, I cry out long

Go head, brother, did you stop to consider?

How it will feel, cold, grinned, grizzly bear jaws

Hot on your heels

Do you stop and whisper, it's Saturday's shore?

The whole world's a savior, who could ever, ever, ever

Ever, ever, ever ask for more?

Do you remember?

Will you stop?

Will you stop?

The pain

And there will never be another one like you

There will never be another one who can do the things you do, oh

Will you give another chance? Will you try little try?

Please stop and you remember, we were together, anyway, all right

How you must of think and wondered, how I must feel

Out on the meadows, while you run the field, I'm alone for you,

And I cry, the sweat, look at it, optical promise, heh, heh, heh,

You'll be dead and in hell, before I'm born, sure thing, brides' maid,

The only solution, isn't it amazing?

Here again are some amazingly prophetic lyrics written and performed by Jim Morrison that suggests "we were together," meaning that I was with Jim in spirit his entire life and helped him write and perform all his music while with The Doors musical group. It's why I was also given the full range of his singing voice as well. Let's first look at "there will never be another one like you, there will never be another one who can do the things you do." What Jim is describing here is my incarnation once conjoined with Jim and the first son, Jesus, how I would then be able to do amazing things via St. Mary and God the Father such as change weather, turn the sun bigger, brighter, and dancing, shooting golden rays, crowning the sun, calling down rainbows, etc. as demonstrated in the first volume of *The New Wine*. Jim used to refer to this phenomenon of us together with this power as being a "monster of energy."

The line "please stop and you remember, we were together" is a direct plea to me in the year 2016 to "stop and remember" that I was with Jim his entire life as spiritually conjoined, immortal, fraternal twin sons of St. Mary, hosting one body. It was important for me to remember this, so I could gather instructions via Jim's lyrics on how to "crack open the gates" and initiate the return of the Christian kingdom. The line "I know your moves, and your mind, and your mind" references how Jim was fully cognizant that it was his half-brother (myself) who was with him in spirit his entire life and that because of how close we are, he knows exactly the way I think and why I choose to do the things that I do for spiritual reasons that have a distinct and defined purpose to fulfill St. Mary's and the Father's agendas.

The lyrics "Go 'head, brother, did you stop to consider? How it will feel, cold, grinned, grizzly bear jaws, hot on your heels" is a reference again to our relationship as actual "brothers" or twins of St. Mary. What

Jim is saying here with the line "cold, grinned grizzly bear jaws hot on your heels" is he is recognizing that as an incarnate Son of St. Mary that I, like him, would be chased by men who are unable to discern a Son of St. Mary from the demonic and this would lead to being constantly hounded by others who are afraid of us and our immortal spiritual conjoining.

I want to focus for a moment now on an amazing photo below. The photo is of the outside of St. Joseph Catholic Church in St. Joseph, Michigan. In the center of the photo, you can see clearly a very bright green orb. There is a similar green orb seen in a photo of the musical group The Doors from the late 1960s with the bandmates all standing outside on a fall day. The green orb in this photo is seen on the left elbow of the late, great Ray Manzarek. I could not enclose that particular photo of The Doors with this green orb present for licensing reasons; however, if you simply go on to YouTube and type in "Shaman's Blues The Doors" and watch the first video that appears showing the members of The Doors all looking at themselves in small round mirrors, you will see the green orb in that music video on YouTube about halfway in. What this green orb represents again is the line "please, stop and you remember, we were together." Again, this references Jim and I being conjoined in one host body with the protection of St. Mary in spirit form in the green orb nearby. A green orb signifies a human spirit that is in total and complete "oneness" with the natural environment. A green orb signifies "love" as well which, as we know from the first volume of *The New Wine*, is one of the keys to the other kingdom.

Photo: St. Joseph Catholic Church in St. Joseph, Michigan. Notice the clearly seen green orb in the middle of the shot. A similar green orb can be seen in the music video for "Shaman's Blues" performed by The Doors musical group on a video on YouTube. The new sun is also shining very brightly and casting its healing rays down from above.

Photo: St. Mary in the stone grotto on a clear sunny day at St. Joseph Catholic Church in St. Joseph, Michigan. Notice again the presence of the green orb at her feet signifying her presence and my spiritual oneness with the natural environment.

Photo: The new sun vibrantly dancing and shimmering on a recent fall evening in October of 2017. Notice again a green orb to the bottom right along with two other multi-colored orbs. The green orb represents the human spirit at oneness in nature and also the presence of St. Mary watching over her conjoined fraternal twins James and Matthew.

Photo: St. Peter inside the chapel at St. Joseph Catholic Church in St. Joseph, Michigan, cloaked in purple holding the two keys to the other kingdom. The two keys are metaphors for entering heaven and are "be love" and "believe."

Blinded by the Light

I can't tell you how many people I know that I've heard say that they can never be around someone that they have had a falling out with ever again because of their hurt pride and anger. If you only knew how much spiritual power is gained by seeking out others you may not like or even think you hate to try to mend the fences. Imagine if everyone on the planet decided to do this? What kind of world would we have?

Consider this undeniable and very disturbing fact: we had a sitting vice-president that personally profited to the tune of $40 million from oil rights gained by his former company of Haliburton during the entire Iraq war. This should be an investigated criminal offense, but it was not. America is no better now than the ancient Roman Empire. It's what Jim sang about with the lyrics "lost in a Roman wilderness of pain and all the children are insane, all the children are insane, waiting for the summer rain." I am praying that The New Wine becomes the summer rain and reign Jim and I sang of.

The lines of "optical promise, heh, heh, heh, you'll be dead and in hell, before I'm born" as well as "will you stop the pain" are also incredibly prophetic. Again, here, Jim references an "optical promise" being made. This is a reference to my finding the "new son" the other half of the "scattered son" being Paxton Elkins through my day job as a sales representative for ophthalmic/optical medical practices in 2016. As I mentioned in the first volume of The New Wine, I would not have encountered Paxton's plight if not for my job as a sales representative for eye surgeons. I was once asked if I "help the blind to see" like Jesus did, and my response is always, "No, more like I help prevent the seeing from going blind." The optical promise here being that I would somehow be able to "stop the pain," both the physical pain of Paxton's DIPG cancer and the emotional pain his family was feeling from his terminal diagnosis. The lines "you'll be dead and in hell before I'm born" is also a prophecy of Jim dying in Paris in 1971, three years before my birth.

The plan from the beginning while I was with Jim in spirit was for him to die and become reincarnated with me to live with me as my spirit guide for our very difficult mission via St. Mary. This plan allowed him to get out of his current situation of being a wrongfully convicted felon in Miami, Florida. As I mentioned in the first volume of The New Wine, I have nearly died five separate times in my life that I can recall. When a son of St. Mary walks the earth, Lucifer/Hillel Ben Shachar/Memnoch/Satan/Red Dragon/Devil knows this as well and will go out of his way to ensure our physical and if possible, spiritual demise. I believe he is the one who attacked young Paxton Elkins with his illness which fulfills a prophecy of "The Woman Clothed in the Sun" which I will discuss later in this book.

This conjoining of Jim and I was also referenced in the popular song written by Bruce Springsteen "Blinded by the Light." In this song covered by Manfred Mann sings "blinded by the light, revved up like a deuce, another runner in the night." This prophetic song written and performed before my birth describes the event I mentioned in the first volume of The New Wine where I was driving in cornfields in rural Michigan and immediately "blinded by light." The "revved up like a deuce" is talking about how my body is host to two (deuce) conjoined souls being James Douglas Morrison and Matthew Douglas Pinard. "Another runner in the night" references the abilities Jim and I have to "play host" to

Lucifer/Hillel Ben Shachar/Memnoch/Satan/Red Dragon/Devil to "run with him in his under lair" of hell or "the night" without being overcome by him. I can host him without allowing him to control or overcome me, and the reason I do this is to gain the advantage of being able to see his plans for this world. Jim recorded a song "End of the Night" that also describes this ability of ours and a foreshadowing of cracking the gates open in the fall of 2016 in order to spiritually "end the night."

\Photo: Matthew Douglas Pinard with Jim and wife, Carol, poking fun at the notion of being the "devil" at a Halloween costume party. I am not the devil at all, but I can play "host" to him to keep him off of others and can "run with him in the night" to try to see his plans for mankind.

Photo: When my late good friend, Randy Godwin, as referenced in the first volume of The New Wine, started visiting me in spirit during the summer of 2016 to help warn me of impending military conflicts, these white orbs with red flares started showing up in most of my photos. Red and white orbs signify both passion and spiritual protection of the highest order. Also, pay close attention to the bottom of the sun where you can see an image of a "second sun" that appears in the middle of the shot. This could also be the red dragon from the prophecy from AD 95 of "The Woman Clothed in the Sun." I needed such protection to give me the strength to help my fraternal twin, James, crack open the gates of heaven in the fall of 2016. James and Randy both are like older brothers in this regard.

Photo: I can't explain precisely what is going on here in this photo; however, it is clearly profoundly spiritual in nature. This also happened around the same time in the fall of 2016 when the "gates were cracked open" during Jim and I's "Indian Summer." Notice as well to the right what appears to be a second sun or perhaps a red orb encircled by a red haze which could be the "red dragon." During my recent prayers to St. Mary, I requested the presence of my Archangels Michael and Gabriel for my protection from Lucifer/Hillel Ben Shachar/ Memnoch/Satan/Red Dragon/Devil. I believe this may be both of my archangels signaling their arrival. Notice how much their brightness overwhelms the red dragon to the right.

Lord of Hosts

Jesus Christ is often referred to as "Lord of hosts." Let me try to explain what this means. As I stated in the first volume of The New Wine, I mentioned being visited by the spirits of friends from my past that I knew to be deceased. The main reason these spirits were visiting me was so that I could both try to warn my country and to warn mutual friends and family of impending dangers on the horizon. Both Jim and I can "host" any spirit or soul that has passed on to the spirit world. This was clearly shown by Oliver Stone in his biopic movie "The Doors." There is a scene where the band is performing the song "Not to Touch the Earth" and you can see Jim Morrison played by actor Val Kilmer dancing on stage during the song as the ghosts of deceased native Americans start dancing on the stage with him. You can see in this clip Ray Manzarek played by actor Kyle MacLachlan actually able to see the spirits himself dancing around Jim Morrison played by actor Val Kilmer as they moved in concert with the music while on stage. I am also quite capable of the same kind of "hosting." What happened with myself, Jim, and first son, Jesus, is best referred to as what I would call "son stacking." That is to say with all of us being now conjoined we have tremendous power and ability and reason.

Photo: The late legendary front man of The Doors, Jim Morrison, performing his "Jesus Christ" pose. This is one of my favorite photos and is often referred to by his fans as "the lion." Jesus is often referred to as "The Lion of Judah." This is around the time that Jim was beginning to play "host" to myself and St. Mary in his own life as the "lions ran in the night." Jim believed he was Dionysus incarnate. He was actually St. Mary's second son and Jesus's half-brother. If you put me in a recording studio today you would hear his voice is now just as powerful. The reason his voice was so powerful was because it was the voice of St. Mary's conjoined fraternal twins singing perfectly in concert together.

Photo: This is Matt (with Jim) circa 1996 in his U.S. Army JAG uniform. Jim used to sing "the blue bus is calling us, come on, baby, take a chance with us," and "kiss the hunter of the green vest who has wrestled before with lions in the night." In basic training, we were driven around in blue buses and in the army, wore green vests with our class A uniforms.

Jim used to refer to our incarnations as "lurking jaws, joints in time." I will expand upon this with a short rhyme that is also a poetic reference to our relationship to each other and our mother. "Lurking jaws, joints in time, three years the time divide, St. Mary's conjoined fraternal twins, her sons divine."

Photo: "The left jaw" James Douglas Morrison high school graduation photo notice the triangular part in the upper right side of his forehead. I have an almost identical part on the opposite side of my forehead.

Photo: "The right jaw" Matthew Douglas Pinard with conjoined fraternal twin James Douglas Morrison thirty years later.

Ghost Light

In the first volume of The New Wine, I relayed a story of when a former friend and fellow actor named Randy Godwin started to visit me. He gave me the words "ghost light" to give to a mutual friend. "Ghost Light" was the title of a television series this friend had been writing, and he hadn't told anyone the name of it yet. I was also able to literally "host" Randy inside my own body. His spirit was able to literally jump inside of me without any discomfort or fear.

When I would ask him a question or ask if I had the message he wanted me to convey correctly, he was actually able to manipulate a part of my injured left shoulder to relieve it temporarily of the chronic arthritic pain I had, so I would know it was him confirming receipt of the message. All throughout Jim's life, he was playing "host" to me, and now I am "hosting" him throughout the rest of my life here on earth. Prior to young Paxton's passing away, it became clear to me that he was starting to learn how to "host" as he was being visited by Archangel Gabriel prior to his death which he described to family as a "blonde man."

Jim and I's mission via St. Mary was to crack open the gates of heaven in the fall of 2016 to try to prevent nuclear war and also to use the 100th anniversary of the Marian apparitions at Fatima to bind Lucifer/Hillel Ben Shachar/ Memnoch/Satan/Red Dragon/Devil permanently to his under lair with our publication of The New Wine series of books. The 100th anniversary of Fatima refers to the 1917 appearance of St. Mary in spirit over the course of six months to three rural farm children in Fatima, Spain, to warn of the dire consequences to all of mankind if there continues to be wars waged on the planet. In order to celebrate and participate in the 100th anniversary of the Fatima apparitions, I had decided to attend a celebration of this event in the summer of 2017 as the first volume of The New Wine was being finalized for publication. The following image below shows the celebration of Fatima I had planned on attending on a Saturday evening, May 13th, 2017, at Sacred Heart Catholic Church in Grand Rapids, Michigan.

Photo: The inside of Sacred Heart Catholic Church in Grand Rapids, Michigan, shown on Saturday, May 13th, 2017, at the 100th anniversary celebration of the Fatima apparitions of St. Mary to farm children in Fatima, Spain. Pay close attention to the white and yellow banners surrounding the altar.

I had a phenomenally intense and revealing mystical experience two days prior to attending the formal mass celebrating the Fatima apparitions. Since I had close family and friends suggesting my recent mystical/spiritual experiences were related to my post-traumatic stress from my military service, I decided for reasons I was unaware of at the time to seek out a professional psychologist trained in hypnotherapy to see if I could ascertain more instruction/direction from St. Mary. The hypnotherapy session was conducted on Thursday, May 11th, 2017, in the afternoon. During the session, I was asked to make a tight closed fist with my right hand as I counted backwards from one hundred to ninety. Pretty soon, I was in a very, very deep hypnotic trance. For some reason, the therapist asked me to envision walking into a temple. He asked me to record in my mind who I met, what I saw, and if I was given anything.

When I finally was called back from the hypnotic trance, I stated that I was inside of what looked like a church with an altar that had white-and-yellow banners hanging around the altar. Immediately upon walking toward the altar, I could distinctly see St. Mary to my left. She held out her hand and summoned for someone to come forward into my view. Immediately, I could see Lucifer/ Hillel Ben Shachar/Memnoch/Satan/Red Dragon/Devil appear from the darkness surrounding us. I will enclose an artist's rendering of what he looks like. He had flickering flames and patches of both bright orange flames and black spots all over his head. As he appeared, he silently handed me a set of "scrolls." St. Mary motioned for him to present the scrolls directly to me and unroll them. The scrolls were completely blank. As I related this set of images to the therapist, he stated that he could also sense I was handed scrolls as well. This is an example of him being connected to my vine during a hypnotherapy session and illustrates the concept "the universal mind" which I will discuss later. When he asked me what I believed it meant, and I stated that Lucifer/ Hillel Ben Shachar/Memnoch/Satan/Red Dragon/Devil has "no response to our New Wine."

After this therapy session, I attended the celebratory mass at Sacred Heart Catholic Church in Grand Rapids, Michigan, on Saturday, May 13th, 2017. After the mass, as I was falling asleep at home in my bed, I woke up with the very distinct sensation of my soul or spirit hovering outside of my body. The only possible word I could think of what was happening was the term "ascension." After Jesus Christ died on the cross and he appeared for forty days afterward, his spirit then ascended into heaven where he remained seated at the right hand of the Father. What was interesting about what was happening to me was it did feel as if my mission was complete. The first volume of The New Wine was about to be published and distributed, and I felt like I had fulfilled the mission of binding Lucifer/Hillel Ben Shachar/Memnoch/Satan/Red Dragon/ Devil at the celebratory mass at Sacred Heart. What happened, however, was I could distinctly feel a heavy hand push me down and back into my body. I knew it was God the Father giving me the distinct message that my job was not yet complete here on earth.

Photo: A statue of St. Mary. This statue resembles very closely the "woman in the veil" who appeared to me during my hypnosis session on Thursday, May 11th, 2017, prior to the celebration of Fatima on Saturday, May 13th, 2017.

Photo: An artist's rendering of Lucifer/Hillel Ben Shachar/Memnoch/Satan/Red Dragon/Devil. This is the closest rendering I've seen to what he looks like in person. You would never want him to appear to you without St. Mary present to help hold him at bay. He has also appeared to me as a dark ram horned like beast as well. This is the entity that appeared to me during my hypnotherapy session on Thursday, May 11th, 2017, as he presented empty scrolls to me.

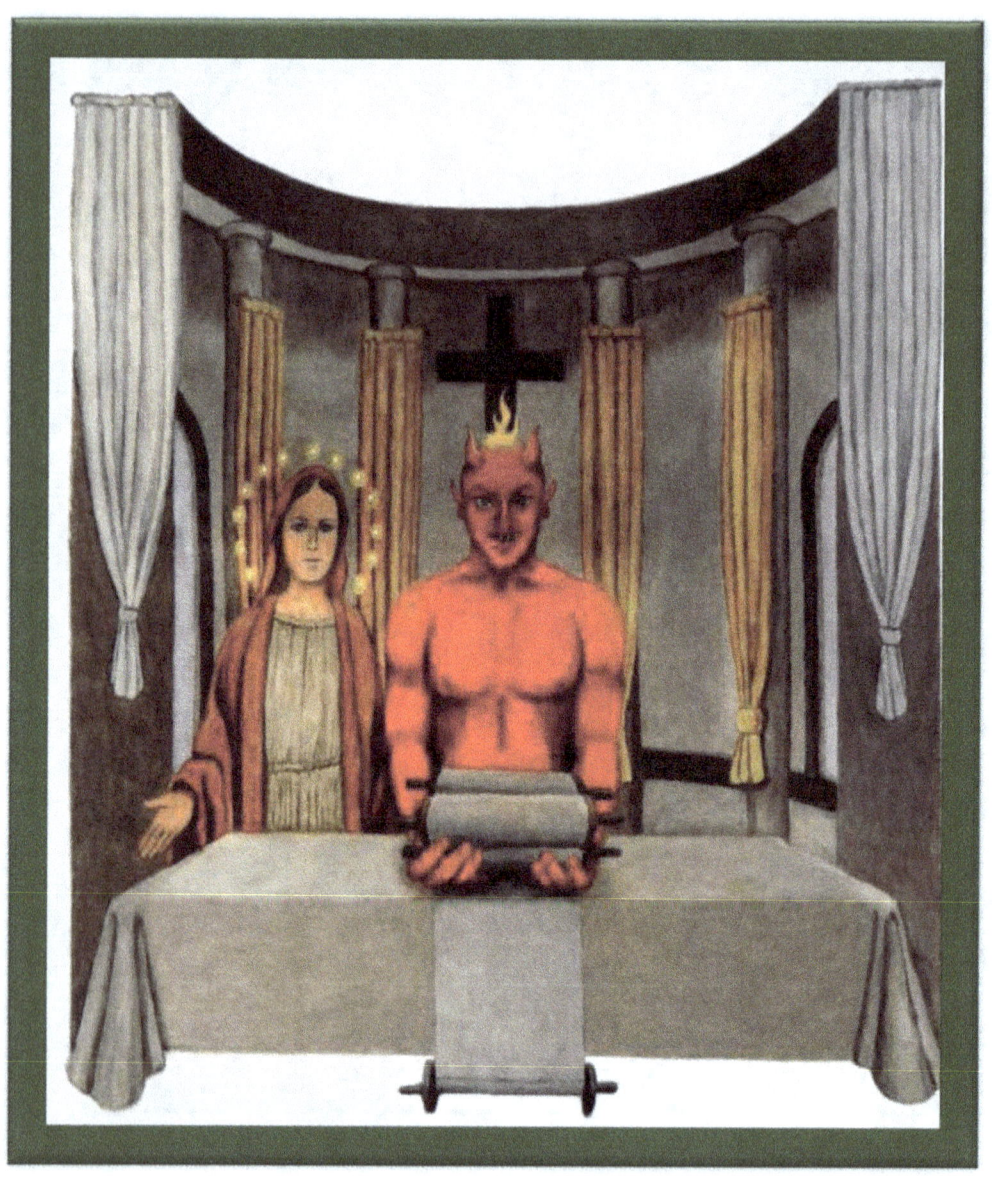

Illustration: Another great illustration from artist Don Williams showing the confrontation on Saturday, May 13th, 2017, between St. Mary and her fraternal twins James and Matthew with Lucifer/Hillel Ben Shachar/Memnoch/Satan/Red Dragon/Devil. Don's amazing artwork can be found at www.donwilliams.daportfolio.com.

Stark Hypnotherapy

The implication of my very vivid and stark hypnotherapy session was quite remarkable. Of note, the first thing I took from this was that by the time I did formally attend the Fatima celebration at Sacred Heart Catholic Church in Grand Rapids, Michigan, on Saturday, May 13th, 2017, the inside of the church which I had never been in nor seen photos of appeared just as it did in the vision of my hypnotherapy session. It was an altar surrounded by white-and-yellow banners. What I believe my session revealed was that as the first volume of The New Wine was being finalized for publication and the Catholic Church was celebrating the 100th anniversary of the Fatima apparitions, St. Mary was indicating that there was an opportunity to bind Lucifer/Hillel Ben Shachar/Memnoch/Satan/Red Dragon/Devil from this earth if both volumes of The New Wine were to be accepted globally by mankind and also if we properly recognized the edicts of the original Fatima message over one hundred years ago of preventing more wars from occurring.

Let me take a moment here to discuss my personal experience with Lucifer/ Hillel Ben Shachar/Memnoch/Satan/Red Dragon/Devil. He is capable of incredibly destructive power, and his ability to manipulate mankind in both thought and deed is quite disturbingly effective. For instance, he is quite capable of grabbing the steering wheel from my hands of the 1990 Ford Taurus my parents bought me for my sixteenth birthday and then force the car sideways into a tree lining a boulevard resulting in a T-bone crash to my driver's side door that paramedics said if it had been twelve inches in another direction I would not have survived. He was capable of making sure the escargot clams I ordered on the deck of a boat restaurant in South Haven, Michigan, a few years ago was poisoned, resulting in my checking in hours later at a local hospital after vomiting every two minutes. He convinced the ER nurse that tried attending to me to deny me a potentially life-saving IV for over an hour while yelling at me in a demonic tone for throwing up in her hospital.

Lucifer/Hillel Ben Shachar/Memnoch/Satan/Red Dragon/Devil is capable of convincing a drill sergeant in the army to jury rig a live hand grenade and make sure it was the one I had in my hands with a faulty pin in it that would explode in my face as I tried to pull it out which very nearly did happen. He was almost capable of convincing the police officer in Indiana who pulled me over a few years ago for "speeding" as I was going eight miles over the speed limit that he should fire his pistol at me through my driver's side window, because he was convinced I was carrying a hand gun in my glove compartment which I was not. He was also quite easily capable of convincing Private Peter Roukis on the army base I was stationed at in 1997 that it was in his best interests to drive two, twin twelve-inch knives through his wife's neck, nearly decapitating her in the process for being unfaithful. He convinced two of my former Christian middle school classmates that the best thing for their lives was to put the barrels of nine-millimeter pistols to their temples and pull the trigger. He is currently convincing twenty military veterans per day to do the same. He is also capable, as I mentioned in the first volume of The New Wine, of convincing a world leader such as Vladimir Putin that it would be a good idea to start a global thermal nuclear war if Americans made a decision in a voting booth that he thought he couldn't live within our 2016 national election.

I have developed a very refined ability to "sense" whenever Lucifer/Hillel Ben Shachar/Memnoch/Satan/Red Dragon/Devil is nearby. Usually, I get a very tight or anxious feeling in my chest. I feel "heavy" and extremely agitated. The way that he "works" you is he will get your mind to focus on something that you may have done that you think is unforgivable and he "rolls you" like a crocodile "roll" its prey. He gets your mind to start skipping like a broken record, so you can't reason your way out. Hell with Lucifer/Hillel Ben Shachar/Memnoch/ Satan/Red Dragon/Devil is the impossibility of reason and a state of constant agitation or irritation. You may notice yourself getting cranky with loved ones or angry and rageful for no reason.

Another ability Lucifer/Hillel Ben Shachar/Memnoch/Satan/Red Dragon/ Devil has is the ability to move from human host to human host via a spiritual phenomenon called "transference." He can do this without actually "possessing" a human body as he can enter your mind and spirit and read your thoughts and also implant thoughts directly into you. He can do this quite easily and even those who have "shored" up on holy sacraments can even sometimes fall victim to this influence. The reason Lucifer/Hillel Ben Shachar/ Memnoch/Satan/Red Dragon/Devil can do these things is at one time he was considered "God's favorite" and was second in command and the top archangel. The name Lucifer means "light bearer," and as such, he was given many abilities to influence mankind to help us all evolve to our best version of God. The problem is he wanted command of the throne. He rebelled against God, and thus, the very gifts he was given to try to help us along in our life journey was instead used to destroy the very creation he hated and feared the most. He is a formidable and terrifying foe.

The best advice I can give is try to learn to discern his voice from my own. For instance, I would never tell you to deliberately harm another person or to deny the existence of God. Lucifer/Hillel Ben Shachar/Memnoch/Satan/Red Dragon/Devil would do such things and so be on guard in your thought life against such spiritual attacks. When he tries to influence you, it is not always as dramatic as a demonic possession with obvious signs like levitations or moving objects across a room. Lucifer/Hillel Ben Shachar/Memnoch/Satan/Red Dragon/Devil is much more subtle. His trick is to make you think you're hearing the voice of God. Jim Morrison and I used to sing live, "I am the lizard king, I can do anything." What he meant by this is that he is king over these "reptilian aliens" and all the extensions of the "other lion in the night" being Lucifer/Hillel Ben Shachar/Memnoch/Satan/Red Dragon/Devil.

Photo: Lucifer/Hillel Ben Shachar/Memnoch/Satan/Red Dragon/Devil is like a crocodile that will "roll" his prey for all of eternity if you allow him to. He wishes to severe you from our garden/other kingdom permanently.

There is a gentleman who has received a lot of press recently named David Icke. Mr. Icke is the author of numerous controversial books describing our global elite world leaders as being possessed by "alien reptilian" entities that wish to enslave us all through senseless wars for profit. He claims these entities live in underground caverns and control things like world militaries and economies. Mr. Icke has been publicly criticized and called "crazy." His theories aren't exactly wrong, however. These entities he is referring to do, in fact, exist, and they are simply extensions of the "other lion in the night" that is known to us as Lucifer/Hillel Ben Shachar/Memnoch/Satan/Red Dragon/Devil. Mr. Icke was also criticized for publicly stating he is the "son" part of the Holy Trinity Godhead. He is not exactly wrong in this regard either. Mr. Icke is simply fulfilling a mission that he has been asked to do by exposing these reptilian entities via the Holy Trinity. He is a very intelligent man who is preaching things like refusing military service which is quite correct to do so. I wish I had taken his advice when I was twenty-two years old before I signed my enlistment papers with the U.S. Army; however, it is my true belief now that even at that difficult time in my life, I was being placed on a direct path via my mother, St. Mary, that would fulfill a specific purpose later on in my life.

After the celebration of the 100th anniversary of Fatima on Saturday, May 13th, 2017, I once again sought out the professional hypnotherapist who put me back under deep hypnosis. The vision I was shown by St. Mary was quite amazing. I was taken to an amusement park and shown what is known as a "round-up ride" where people are strapped into a circular rotating cage that spins around rapidly. I saw hundreds even thousands of images of human bodies/souls inside this cage. As the cage started to rotate faster and faster, a large white-winged dove appeared above the cage as it started flapping its large wings. The souls of the people inside the ride started flying up into the sky as if they were inside the vortex of a tornado or water spout. I truly believe St. Mary was saying that the recent celebration of the Catholic mass at Sacred Heart Catholic Church helped to free the souls of many dearly departed up into heaven for all of eternity. It was an intensely comforting image and not one of distress at all.

Illustration: Another amazing illustration by artist Don Williams of the "round-up ride" vision I had while under hypnosis showing a white-winged dove fanning human souls into the "wheel in the sky." Don's amazing artwork can be found at www.donwilliams.daportfolio.com.

At present, we are seeing major changes in weather, globally devastating earthquakes, never before seen record-setting-sized hurricanes, tsunamis, and stark extreme changes in water levels and purities. We are, no doubt, in the Book of Revelations. I want to at this time address the "third secret or seal of the Fatima prophecies." This third seal or secret was so disturbing in its predictions that the pope sealed its facts for many, many years. As I understand it to be the third seal or secret discusses the "rising of a second sun" and the approach of a "red dragon" planet that many refer to as Wormwood/Nibiru/Planet X/Nemesis. It describes a great "fire from the sky" that will wipe out two thirds of the world's population. Such a great fire could be from either nuclear war or from a planetary collision.

NASA has publicly denied the existence of this second sun for many years but now is publicly stating that it does exist and also has seven orbiting planets surrounding it. This planetary system was also prophesied by both Jim Morrison and his drummer, John Densmore, in The Doors song, "Love Her Madly." In the song, Jim sings of "seven horses" that "seem to be on the mark." The seven horses referenced here are the seven orbiting planets of the Nibiru system. The Ancient Sumerians also described Nibiru as a red or brown dwarf star system that circles our solar system every 3,600 years or so, often bringing destruction to the planet from its large mass and gravitational pull that results in our poles shifting and extreme weather patterns that are destructive. I have seen many, many convincing photos and videos of this Nibiru system on YouTube and Google. I have to admit I was extremely skeptical of this alleged second sun and its orbiting planets until my wife and her friend took a photo of the following image near our beaches on Grand Haven, Michigan, in the fall of 2017. I was coincidentally around the same time getting vivid images from St. Mary showing me the earth's crust being ripped up and massively huge tsunamis crashing ashore.

Photo: This photo was taken by my wife in the fall of 2017 and shows what appears to be two suns in our skies. I do not believe this to be a "sun dog" or reflection or a "blood moon." The red dragon or Nibiru planetary system is to the right in this frame in my opinion. You can see this second sun is partially covered by clouds which further suggests this is not a reflection or "sun dog."

Nibiru System

If this Nibiru system is headed toward our planet bringing potential destruction with it, it does not seem to be a coincidence that this is happening at a time when our nation appears to be headed toward a possible second Korean war that could turn to a global nuclear war. It is also interesting how this star system is approaching on the 100th anniversary of the Fatima apparitions warning mankind of the dire consequences of continuing to wage war on the planet.

I also want to take a moment to identify a number of half-breeds. What I mean by this is St. Mary and I have brought into the world a number of half-human/halves Anunnaki angels. Most of them have ended up in the entertainment industry and this is not by mistake. They would show high aptitudes in not only intelligence tests, but also the arts. Most of them have dark facial features and also "holy moles" on their faces. The names I can disclose for certain as being Anunnaki "half-breeds" are Tom Cruise, Al Pacino, Robert De Niro, Michael Madsen, Matt Dillon, Billy Zane, Jim Caviezel, Jennifer Connelly, Demi Moore, Matthew McConnaughey, Colin Farrell, Keanu Reeves, Jason Patric, Billy Crudup, Kate Beckinsale, Rachel Weisz, Madeleine Stowe, Bridget Moynahan, Ben Affleck, Matt Damon, Patrick Wilson, Gal Gadot, Alicia Vikander, Kevin Costner, Jeff Daniels, Oliver Stone, Eddie Vedder, Alanis Morisette, Jon Bon Jovi, Ritchie Sambora, Elvis Presley, Steven Tyler, Joe Perry, Chris Cornell, Dave Navarro, Perry Farrell, Saul Hudson (Slash), Brandi Carlile, and Tom Kiefer. I suspect there could be more, but I am not sure.

I actually had a recent experience where I sensed that Lucifer/Hillel Ben Shachar/Memnoch/Satan/Red Dragon/Devil was attacking one of these famous celebrities who is also coincidentally an Oscar winner. This particular celebrity was not in any kind of "sin" and is considered a great person with a wonderful family. Her life actually also fulfills a prophecy from a song written by Sugarloaf in 1970 entitled, "Green Eyed Lady." This actress has green eyes and was also born in 1970 and is described in the song as "Passion's Lady."

Photo: The band Sugarloaf's "Green Eyed Lady" from the song of the same title written and recorded in 1970 is none other than Oscar winner Jennifer Connelly who coincidentally also has the initials of "J.C." Jen would have amazing abilities to be clairvoyant, host spirits, see past and future events, and decipher and decode complex riddles/poems/prophecies, change weather forecasts, etc. She (like Jesus Christ) is an Anunnaki "half-breed" identifiable by her dark features and "holy moley" on her left top lip.

Green Eyed Lady

What was insidious was when I sensed this particular actress was being targeted, I asked the entity to show its face to me and to tell me its name. The name I was given was "Memnoch." In fact, "Memnoch, The Devil" was the name of a book published by author Anne Rice and it is certainly one of Satan's monikers that he uses to confuse potential targets/hosts. Lucifer will change names often to seem innocuous or to stoke curiosity in its potential target/host. I commanded the entity by its name to stop harassing and trying to influence or possess this particular actress.

Lucifer/Hillel Ben Shachar/Memnoch/Satan/Red Dragon/Devil is incredibly devious and very difficult to subdue in his constant quest to destroy mankind. This is exactly why I published the first volume of The New Wine. I wish to curb anymore suicides by celebrities who may not realize how easily they could spiritually protect themselves. I personally was very upset by the suicide of Chris Cornell who died five days after I attended the Fatima celebration in May of 2017, and I wish he would have had a copy of my book and would have called someone if he was struggling. I was a great fan of his music and I was very angry that Lucifer/Hillel Ben Shachar/Memnoch/Satan/Red Dragon/Devil targeted him and ultimately was responsible for his death in my opinion.

These individuals would have enormous spiritual abilities to not only conjoin and commune with myself and St. Mary, but they would be incarnate angels of light that would have incredible powers if properly unlocked. What's quite fascinating, actually, is the relationship Jim Morrison has with Alanis Morisette. I have never met her, but her voice is clearly not from this earth. She also was born within months of myself as well in 1974. If you combine the names Morrison and Morisette, you get "mori-son-sette" or (more sunsets). St. Mary has quite a sense of humor when it comes to her flock.

Most of these individuals have dark skin and would have moles on their face (holy moley) and would have very incredible spiritual potentials. They would be able to affect the weather, see past events to determine what happened (i.e. a crime scene), predict future events, have heightened senses of impending danger, and be able to commune with other angels and saints from the garden of Eden. Other artists and humans that would have more fair skin or Nordic features but with the presence of moles on the face would be considered Pleiadeans. These are also half human spiritually speaking and would also have very benevolent characteristics of protecting and helping advance the human race.

I had a very interesting experience recently this past summer of 2017 as well that was somewhat alarming. I was out in my neighborhood walking my dogs prior to leaving to the other "west coast" of Los Angeles to promote the release of the first volume of The New Wine. As I walked down my street, I saw a very large black-winged eagle flying overhead. It seemed quite out of place and it soon disappeared. I looked up online and that species is quite rare for the area I live in in West Michigan. When I looked online what the spiritual meaning of this could be, it said a black eagle is often a harbinger or messenger of impending doom. I hope that I am wrong about this.

Illustration: A similar looking and very large black eagle was spotted in my neighborhood this past summer of 2017. These types of birds have been known to be harbingers or messengers of impending doom.

So, what can any of us do? I will tell you what I do as my daily prayer regimen. I say an entire Rosary of Hail Mary's every day now. There are five decades or sets of ten prayers on each Rosary. My favorite places to do this are St. Mary's Catholic Church in Spring Lake, Michigan, and St. Joseph Catholic Church in St. Joseph, Michigan. In the first volume of The New Wine, I enclosed a photo of St. Mary inside the church at St. Joseph Catholic Church in St. Joseph, Michigan. As I was praying there one day, I had a parishioner ask me why I choose to come to this church in spite of having a Catholic church five minutes from my home. My initial answer was for some reason, the statue of St. Mary inside the church is extremely powerful. The parishioner stated that this particular statue is covered with the famed French soldier's fleur-de-lis instead of the usual sun bursts.

Image: The French soldier's fleur-de-lis covers the statue of St. Mary in the chapel of St. Joseph Catholic Church in St. Joseph, Michigan. This is the crest coincidentally that was also used by my military unit while I was on active duty in the 4/2 Armored Cavalry Unit of the U.S. Army. The motto of our unit was "Toujours pret" which translates to "Always ready."

Photo: A statue of St. Mary holding the baby Jesus inside St. Joseph Catholic Church in St. Joseph, Michigan. Notice the golden fleur-de-lis or French soldiers flower covering her blue robe.

Photo: The statue of St. Mary inside St. Joseph Catholic Church in St. Joseph, Michigan, wearing her blue robe covered with the French soldier's fleur-de-lis flowers. To her side is the hanging body of the first son, Jesus Christ. Notice the spear wound on the statue of Jesus Christ also shows the fatal piercing wound to be on his right side. This is also incorrect as the spear wound was on top of his left rib cage where the heart would be. As I mentioned in the first volume of The New Wine, I have a birthmark that appears as a stab wound above the top of my left rib cage.

Photo: An incredible image taken during the summer of 2017 in West Michigan showing the full lunar/solar eclipse that occurred ushering in our new sun and new moon.

Photo: Another incredible sunset photo taken in the summer of 2017, showing a glimpse of the other kingdom off the beaches near Ferrysburg, Michigan.

Photo: This incredible photo shows a veiled woman's face above the sun. The apparition of St. Mary fulfills a Prophecy of "The Woman Clothed with the Sun" from AD 95.

The photograph from above, as first shown in the first volume of The New Wine, shows St. Mary's veiled face above the sun. This apparition fulfills a prophecy from AD 95 of "The Woman Clothed with the Sun." If you look closely above, you will see her face is above the sun which seems to then "clothe" the rest of her. Some people who have seen this photo also claim to see her arms or wings outstretched to both sides. The prophecy describes this woman as the "Woman of the Apocalypse" as prophesied in the Book of Revelations, chapter 12. In this narrative, the woman gives birth to a male child that is attacked by the red dragon identified as Lucifer/Hillel Ben Shachar/ Memnoch/Satan/Red Dragon/Devil. When the child is taken to heaven, the woman flees into the wilderness leading to a "war in heaven," in which the angels cast out the red dragon. Lucifer/Hillel Ben Shachar/Memnoch/Satan/ Red Dragon/Devil then attacks the woman, who is given wings to escape (think back to the photo of Archangel Gabriel's wings shown earlier in this book), and then attacks her again with a flood of water from his mouth (massive tsunamis), which is subsequently swallowed by the earth (massive earthquakes).

Frustrated, the red dragon initiates war on "the remnant of her seed" identified as the righteous followers of Jesus Christ. Recently, as I was praying to St. Mary to "show me" where Lucifer/Hillel Ben Shachar/Memnoch/Satan/Red Dragon/Devil was presently at, I was shown a set of flashing images that ended up being quite prophetic. First, I was shown an owl, a gray wolf behind a cage, and an African deer with antlers. The implication I took away from this was that Lucifer/Hillel Ben Shachar/Memnoch/Satan/Red Dragon/Devil was now bound to only hosting/influencing animals. The second set of images I received was fire being ejected from the earth's crust as in a volcanic eruption. A few days after, I put together an email summarizing these images that I sent to my local parish priest Fr. Dave Gross, a volcano erupted in Japan that had been dormant for over 250 years. A few weeks after that eruption, a Hawaiian volcano erupted that carried fields of lava into residential neighborhoods. A few days after the Japan and Hawaii volcanoes a third volcano then erupted in Guatemala. Sometimes, our "Sun dome" has to resort to using powerful natural forces to combat the incredible negative energy of Lucifer/Hillel Ben Shachar/Memnoch/Satan/Red Dragon/Devil.

All of these fits perfectly with the events of the fall of 2016 up until the fall of 2017. In the fall of 2016, I had a very intense experience while walking into one of my eye doctor's offices. I encountered an elderly woman who had literally incurred a very nasty "fall" outside of the medical office. Her chin had a nasty open gash underneath it which resulted in thick, viscous blood which was dripping from her chin. The blood was not normal and reminded me of descriptions of the blood from Jesus's "Passion" and it happened in "the fall" or "autumn" season which could also reference "the fall of mankind" in original sin. It was so alarming I put together a memo describing the event and sent it on to some Catholic priests I've known my entire life.

Coincidentally, I had just finished completing a writer's workshop at The Purple Rose Theatre Company in Chelsea, Michigan, and wrote a ten-page short play entitled The Fall, which was critically well-received. This particular event with this elderly woman to me was very alarming and seemingly prophetic.

The prophecy of the Woman of the Apocalypse also notes a child of St. Mary being taken to heaven (whom I believe to be Paxton Elkins) and a resulting "war" with the remnants of the righteous followers of Jesus Christ and Lucifer taking place. This certainly would line up with the current state or the world being on the brink of a potential new Korean war and possible global nuclear war. This is why I pray, at minimum, one full Rosary per day in front of a statue of St. Mary. I feel it is the only thing any of us can do at the present moment in a world where nations continue to spend trillions on real weapons of mass destruction that are capable of destroying all life on this planet. When I pray to St. Mary, I say to her "in shalla, mama" which means "God be with you and the Father's will be done on earth," and then I simply ask for her to show me what specifically she wants me to do for her and my Father for that day. I also ask her to "send down my Father's white-winged dove" to "fill the children with his agape love" so that there is no more war on earth.

I want to share now a very profound and quite personal story that I think will further highlight how "death makes angels of us all and gives us wings as smooth as raven's claws" and how each and every one of us is ultimately an angel from the other kingdom. A few years ago, I hesitantly took a new sales job with an eye care company that required my wife and our adopted son and our two dogs to move to Westfield, Indiana, for one year to work for the new company. While we were down there, our adopted son had gotten into some trouble with his school for bringing a knife to class one day. We found out that he was getting bullied at school and thought he needed it for protection.

Thankfully, the school officials did not expel him, and he was not introduced into the adult criminal justice system. They instead referred us to a local psychologist who gave both my son and I much needed psychotherapy. Upon disclosing both my son's history of abuse and my traumatic experiences from the army and from my neighbor that I referenced in the first volume of The New Wine, who was a very dangerous pedophile I was asked to testify against, this particular female therapist stated, "I know this is going to sound odd, but I was supposed to meet you." When I asked her why she believed that, she did not have an answer other than it seemed just like "one of those things."

Months later, after my family moved back to West Michigan while I was still with the same company, I stopped into the adoration chapel at St. Joseph Catholic Church in St. Joseph, Michigan, and to my utter shock and amazement, as I gazed up at the painting of Jesus Christ carrying his cross surrounded by a few praying angels, I noticed something quite extraordinary. The painting of the female angel as shown below that is to the top left of the painting of Jesus looks almost exactly like the face of the female psychotherapist that assisted my family in Indiana a few years ago.

It was as if the artist was channeling this woman's image who is a very real professional female therapist living and working in Indiana to help those who've suffered past abuse and trauma. I don't think she quite realizes that she is an incarnate angel from the other kingdom, but she knew that she was supposed to meet me in her life as a therapist. What was amazing was during one of my psychotherapy sessions, one particular exercise we did seemed to "unlock" my abilities to receive spiritual communication from the other kingdom like never before. It was no doubt why we were supposed to meet on this side, and it was predetermined many, many years ago, prior to either of our births.

Photo: The inside of the adoration chapel in St. Joseph Catholic Church in St. Joseph, Michigan. The female angel to the top left with wings spread open resembles an actual woman I encountered who is an exceptionally talented and clairvoyant psychotherapist in Indiana. I believe the artist, who no doubt has never met this woman was somehow seeing her face in his mind as he painted this many, many years ago.

    I want to now make a few comments on the topic of "spiritual warfare" and receiving instruction/communication via the other kingdom. I highly recommend if you choose to join St. Mary and I in our battle against the dark one to seek out St. Mary in your prayers. I say this for a number of reasons. Number one, many people often confuse the sons of Mary (Jim and I for instance) with Lucifer simply for the reason that both energies are distinctly male and that Lucifer can often be found lurking near us to try to disrupt our mission and isolate us from others. Both Jim and I have been accused of being the devil simply for this reason. There is nothing Lucifer/Hillel Ben Shachar/ Memnoch/Satan/Red Dragon/Devil would love more than to destroy a son of St. Mary. Sometimes, it can be difficult to discern the difference in male spirit energies, and thus the confusion of any message you would have received would be difficult to discern.

    I have been battling Lucifer/Hillel Ben Shachar/Memnoch/Satan/Red Dragon/Devil for many, many thousands of years. I understand some will question this claim, that to me is immaterial at this very critical juncture in human history. I have many repressed memories of being stabbed by a spear while on a cross on my left side, and thus also have a birthmark atop my left rib cage as I stated in the first volume of The New Wine. I also know I have a half brother named James who I also know as my fraternal twin of St. Mary. I was with him in his most present incarnation as Jim Morrison, lead singer of The Doors musical group. These are simple truths that I do not even question. Some people may read this and will not be able to agree with these truths and that is okay. Although since the second key is "believe," it will make it much more difficult to enter the other kingdom without doing so.

    If you wish to help us in our spiritual battle against the dark one, I recommend a few things. You can always contact me, and I will leave my personal cell phone and email in this edition as well. You can always contact a local Catholic priest or nun and ask questions about how to receive holy sacraments if you've never had them. I personally can simply use holy water and a simple Rosary and talk directly to my mother St. Mary in a church and receive instructions from her, but again, I was raised Catholic from birth so there's a strong bond there. I don't have all the answers all the time. I usually get a sense or intuition if I am being asked to be somewhere or to do something for her. Sometimes, I need others to assist me as well.

Recently, this past fall of 2017, my wife and I started having some very intense type of poltergeist activity in our home. The photo below shows a wooden and metal gold cross we have sitting on our mantle above our fire place. On two separate occasions this cross flew straight across the room while both my wife and I witnessed this strange phenomenon. A few days after this happened, my wife was taking a shower and called me in distress because she noticed three very distinct and very long scratches appear on the side of her leg. A few days later, we asked our parish priest Father Dave to come bless the house.

These events neither surprise me nor do they frighten me. I know exactly who it is. It is Lucifer/Hillel Ben Shachar/Memnoch/Satan/Red Dragon/Devil trying to intimidate me and frighten me from further publications of The New Wine and from trying to help others find help from St. Mary and myself and all our angels and saints.

Yes, I do believe we are in End Times or the Apocalypse or the Book of Revelations which all reference the same thing. As I stated in the first volume of The New Wine this all could simply mean a return to worship and trust in God the Father and The Holy Trinity. Personally, I would like to "end time" in a different way. Allow me to explain, what puts us in early graves is this incessant focus on "time management." Think about this for a moment, we Americans work longer and harder for much less pay than most of Europe. That's not to mention how indigent and poor South American and Asian countries are and how much time they spend toiling away in sweat shops for pennies. This world is owned and run by the ultra-wealthy, the top 1 percent who wish to enslave us. Jim and I used to sing about this enslavement when we sang in the song Five to One with the line "trading your hours for a handful of dimes."

I've personally witnessed close family spend over thirty years or more toiling away working sixty or seventy-hour weeks, having multiple heart attacks just to simply provide the basics. This is not how God intended this world to be. An "end to time" could mean living your life the way God intended for you to be happy, free, with many spiritual riches that are not just material things. As Jim and I once sang in the song "The Soft Parade," you all should simply trust and believe in and "kiss the hunter of the green vest who has wrestled before with lions in the night." This is a reference to my prior U.S. Army service (a hunter in a green vest), who has experience battling someone as deceptive and powerful as the "lion in the night" being Lucifer/Hillel Ben Shachar/Memnoch/Satan/ Red Dragon/Devil.

Photo: This very heavy and rather large wooden and gold cross flew across our living room on two separate occasions. I'm certain it was Lucifer/Hillel Ben Shachar/Memnoch/Satan/Red Dragon/Devil trying to threaten and intimidate my publications of volumes I and II of The New Wine. Trust me, he does not want anyone attached to our new vine via our new wine.

Photo: This is the "blood, blood, blood" dripping from the "Pirate Prince" at "her (St. Mary's) side" mural painting of the first son, Jesus Christ, in our St. Mary's Catholic Church in Spring Lake, Michigan. Jim and I sang about this mural painting in the song "Wild Child."

Photo: This remarkable statue can be found at St. Paul's Catholic Church in Valparaiso, Indiana. The banner above references the "two keys" first introduced in the first volume of The New Wine. It specifically focuses on the key of "believe." Believe in yourself, your fellow man, and the Holy Trinity.

Photo: An incredible sunset from St. Mary in the skies of West Michigan in the Summer of 2017. Notice the bands of yellow, orange, and red hues. Jim referred to this as a "rich mandala for me and you."

Photo: A stark sunset in West Michigan in the summer of 2017. St. Mary is showing off the red radiance of the two merged kingdoms.

Photo: This amazing photo was taken in December of 2017 after I had prayed for three hours at St. Mary's Catholic Church in Spring Lake, Michigan, for St. Mary to show the entire world with The New Wine publications who her conjoined fraternal twin sons are (James and Matthew) and for Paxton to rejoin us one day.

Photo: This amazing photo was taken the day I accepted the final edits to my second book in Paxton's honor. The sunset is almost identical to the one above that was taken on December of 2017 following Paxton's passing away. This was a sign from St. Mary that my publishing this book in Paxton's honor of him being an incarnate Son of St. Mary is the truth behind his very short, yet meaningful life.

Photo: The new sun shining brightly from above down over trees in our backyard in Spring Lake, Michigan, in the summer of 2017. Notice again the presence of three multi-colored orbs surrounded by a purple ring or haze.

Photo: The new sun shining brightly in Western Michigan skies in the summer of 2017. Notice again bright orange-and-yellow bands surrounding a very bright center.

Photo: The bright new sun shining in the skies near Copper Harbor, Michigan, in the upper peninsula. Notice again how it is not spherical but appears as three merged spheres. My wife and I took this trip in mid July 2017, and the locals stated it was the first few days that year that far north where the weather was over 80 degrees with the sun visible.

Photo: A rich exploding sunset of dark red, orange, and yellow bands off the coast of Grand Haven State Park in the summer of 2017. The other kingdom is a "sun dome in the night."

Photo: A remarkable shot of the new sun vibrantly showing rays pointing again to the two kingdoms of heaven and earth in the summer of 2017. Notice how the light waves emanating from the center look like "angel wings."

Photo: An incredible "buffalo-head-looking" cloud formation. It appears to look like a buffalo looking off to the right with a large hump on its back. This was granted to me by St. Mary based on the poem Jim and I wrote in my teens entitled "Buffalo," as printed in the first volume of The New Wine.

Photo: A Great Plains wild buffalo with his "goateed cranium the size of a globe."

Buffalo

Massive

Graceful

Goateed cranium the size of a globe

Gather the hunt for the torch party

Ripped and stretched

Tight and torn

Fat hooves beat the earth as drum

Eroded and repentant the gated ground consents

To have and to hold the bit and reins which tie the gums

I found a new breed for domestication

Wild hair of brown burning fire Comfort coat of winter night

Matthew Douglas Pinard and James Douglas Morrison

Photo: This incredible photo was taken near dusk by my wife, and it appears to be a mother holding her infant child. This was a clear message to me from St. Mary that all our prayers regarding young Paxton Elkins had been heard from above. It was also a message to my wife showing how Paxton and myself with Jim are part of St. Mary's "scattered sons."

Photo: Another incredible sunset in West Michigan in the summer of 2017 showing again the golden rays from the other kingdom.

Photo: A remarkable gold and wood statue of the first son, Jesus Christ, nailed to the cross outside of Sacred Heart Catholic Church in Grand Rapids, Michigan, on Saturday, May 13th, 2017, prior to the 100th anniversary mass and celebration of the Fatima apparitions of St. Mary.

I want to, for a moment, focus on the issue of public preaching. I personally listen to a lot of Christian radio programs when driving around in West Michigan. While there are some very good faith-based programs out there, there is also a lot of misinformation being put out there. Part of the other reason I am here is to help clarify a lot of the messages from thousands of years ago. Some of those preaching's given by the first son, Jesus Christ, were designed for the specific times and purposes. For instance, things that were attributed to spiritual purity such as diet, sexual morality, and how to pray were all discussed by Jesus at a time that was very different in world history.

Personally, I dislike words like "preach, evangelize, or convert," since they have, in my mind, come to be associated with negative connotations of something being forced upon you. I mentioned in the first volume of The New Wine the concept of "shepherding" which is a very dangerous and deceitful practice of a religious leader, shepherding out anyone that opposes them or does not believe in them to be a true messenger of God.

I was born into what has now been defined as a "cult" by numerous professionals in the mental health industry. The cult I was born into was called The Word of God/Sword of the Spirit, and it was founded in the mid-1960s. I personally believe this group was founded on a genuine interest in knowing and following God. As often happens, however, is once this kind of pursuit of "light" occurs, Lucifer is there to try to disrupt this connection. Consequently, the cult I grew up in began to deliberately use the principles of shepherding/discipleship. Some of the instruction from this cult was based in goodness and was sound advice such as seeking out the Holy Spirit in prayer and learning to discern Lucifer/Hillel Ben Shachar/Memnoch/Satan/Red Dragon/Devil from Jesus and St. Mary.

While there were many very decent and loving people that were in this cult that I consider to be quality individuals, there were those that simply wanted authority and control over others and sought to use cult like tactics to assert dominion over its members. I discovered documents from those days that were drafted by the leader of this cult in which he mandated that anyone in the cult must refer to him as "the dictator," and he also listed many bizarre rules such as a wife must never deny her husband sexual relations, and a husband is not allowed in the delivery room as his wife went through labor. The cult even had a middle school I attended from fourth to eighth grade. The teachers of this school mandated that girls and boys could never speak to each other and jeans and rock music were prohibited. Boys had to wear ties and girls had to wear plaid skirts.

Many "problem" children were taken into the basement of the school and beaten with wooden paddles as punishment that sometimes caused major welts on the back of the children's legs. Some of us tried to threaten calling the police and authorities to inform them of the physical abuse but were further chastised by the adults who ran the school to never do so under the threat of further punishments. I, like many of my classmates, was singled out as a "troublemaker" by teachers and suffered anxiety and depression for many years in the teens as a result of this abuse. As I mentioned earlier, two of my former classmates are now dead from suicide. Many of the Word of God cult leaders also tried to petition the Catholic Church to ordain them as married lay people and stated how they enjoyed dinners at the Vatican served on gold plates. The Word of God cult disbanded in the early 1990s when I was still in high school, after numerous warnings from Catholic bishops about these invasive practices and abuses of power. Some of these adults to this day deny any of these things occurred, and some are still, to this day, publicly preaching Christianity while still denying their role in any of this abuse of children.

These are tactics that Lucifer/Hillel Ben Shachar/Memnoch/Satan/Red Dragon/Devil likes to use to convince others that they are actually hearing God's voice and carrying out his will, when, in effect, they are fulfilling the agenda of the dark one. If someone is going to be in public ministry, I believe there must be some kind of vetting process and public transparency, as well as formal ministerial training. As I stated before, if you truly wish to assist St. Mary and I in our extremely difficult mission of binding Lucifer/Hillel Ben Shachar/Memnoch/Satan/Red Dragon/Devil to his under lair, then I recommend seeking her out in your daily prayers. This can also be done in private or through a minister or Catholic priest. As I said before, I simply ask her every day what it is she wishes for me to do that day for her and our Father. She is here as the mother of all of us and is more than willing to help you discern what is truly the direction coming from our other kingdom versus what is coming from the dark one.

As I mentioned in the first volume of The New Wine, Jim prophesized he and I's incarnation/conjoining in West Michigan in the song "The End" as he sang "ride the snake to the lake, the ancient lake." The ancient lake being a reference to Lake Michigan near my West Michigan home, and also, the "snake" being he and I conjoined as a seventy-year-old "serpent." This allusion to sons of St. Mary being "serpents" is not anything new. In fact, the image below of St. John showing a serpent coming out of the chalice where the Blood of Christ is kept is also an allusion to the same thing. Most Christians associate the image of the serpent as being that exclusively associated with Lucifer/Hillel Ben Shachar/Memnoch/Satan/Red Dragon/Devil. The truth is St. Mary has her own "serpent" who is far greater in power and who can offer followers much more than Lucifer promises which is an eternal life of freedom. We should be embraced as Jim used to sing "ride the snake, to the lake, the ancient lake, baby." A similar image of a snake coming out of a chalice can be found in the stained-glass windows above the altar at St. Patrick's Catholic Church in Grand Haven, Michigan.

Image: St. John showing the image of a "serpent" coming out of the chalice that represents the "Blood of Christ." This serpent is not Lucifer or Satan, rather, it is her conjoined fraternal twin sons James and Matthew (Jesus/True King).

I want to take some time here to discuss a very sensitive situation that deeply affected me personally and also had the potential to deeply impact the national security of our country and potentially lead to a very destructive global conflict. In my time as a sales representative for an eye care company calling on eye surgeons for a living, I encountered an older surgeon that soon became a very close friend of mine due to our shared military service backgrounds. This gentleman claimed to be recruited into the CIA in the early 1980s and was deliberately sent to ophthalmology school to be trained as an eye surgeon so he could as he put it "cross any border in the world with no questions asked."

I soon developed quite a lasting friendship with this fascinating individual, and we would have dinner at least once a month in Traverse City, Michigan, for a number of years. He relayed very fascinating stories of some of his covert missions which was intriguing and entertaining. What made this situation extremely sensitive is the last dinner I had with him, he told me he had fallen in love with a Chinese woman who was in Michigan to write a story for a Chinese paper on the Interlochen Music Academy in northern Michigan. Within a few months of a whirlwind romance, this man was soon engaged to this Chinese woman. I now suspect she was probably a mole and an MSS agent for the Chinese military. He told me they had planned to live on his farm in Traverse City, Michigan, and he was going to finish out his days as a surgeon in the area.

At my last dinner with this man, he, out of the blue, told me he was moving immediately to Beijing, China, which I found to be odd because I know how much he loved Traverse City. What was odd was at our dinner, he kept goading me to come visit him in China, and that "I would love it there." I believe he knew my true spiritual identity and that he was also very clairvoyant himself. It was like he was trying to tell me something without directly telling me. He then proceeded to inform me about the first time he met his future wife's brother who "coincidentally" was also a Chinese Red Army General. This was not unusual, but what he told me next was. He said that as he sat in front of this Chinese Red Army General, he pulled out a large file at least six inches thick that detailed every single covert operation my friend had performed as a covert CIA agent for over thirty years.

Now as a former Army JAG service member with a graduate degree in military history, this last piece of information was extremely alarming. The implications are quite disturbing. This means that the Chinese who in the last two years have been conducting unprecedented joint naval exercises in the South China Sea with Russia have somehow penetrated our military and intelligence agencies to the point of being able to extract covert intelligence from over thirty years of operations. They should never, ever have access to such sensitive information.

I was so disturbed by this I ended up personally calling Langley, Virginia, at CIA headquarters to report a possible forced defection to an enemy country that has developed the ability to compromise our highly classified intelligence files. The investigator I spoke with said directly to me, "With your JAG background, you realize our mission, and this is the exact kind of thing we worry about." He told me he was going to follow up with me a few days later if he was able to "gain any traction" on this potential internal breach. What happened two weeks later was incredibly disturbing. I called CIA headquarters again and asked to speak to the same investigator. When I called, I was told that he had been placed on "indefinite administrative leave."

This was highly unusual and potentially indicative of a massive breach of our internal security at the highest levels of both military and our intelligence services that our government did not want made public. In fact, soon after my phone call, I read in a major newspaper that we had been hiding from the general public the fact that the Russians have been able to hack our electrical grid, and the Chinese have been able to penetrate our intelligence agencies for quite a few years; a fact not clearly known to the general American public. All of this happened in the fall of 2016 and subsequently led me to seek out cracking open the gates in West Michigan as I demonstrated in the first volume of The New Wine to fulfill all of Jim's prophecies and bring down the other kingdom's archangels and saints.

My point is this: we have a world now where multiple countries have large arsenals of thousands of high tech weapons capable of destroying life on this planet many times over within thirty to forty-five minutes of a launch. We, as humans, have reached a time in history where the future of this planet now rests in the hands of non-Christian and very ruthless leaders who have defined agendas of fulfilling the interests of the top 1 percent of wealthy individuals, many of which hold high positions in our governments. We also have now a very profit driven military industrial complex that we were warned of by presidents like Ike Eisenhower. This is not what this planet was intended for. The question I pose in general to all of mankind is does anyone want to live long term in this kind of constant threat all the time?

After this incident with my close former CIA friend, who I had lost email contact with and wondered if he was still alive, I also myself began to fear for my own life not trusting the CIA to "follow back up with me" as I had just reported a very potential high-level leak on an open phone line. I recall stating to my wife if I were to be found dead from a "suicide" that it was no such thing. As it pertains again to Jim's prophecies and this time period in the fall of 2016, I want to quote his lines from the song "The Unknown Soldier." In this song, he sings, "Wait until the war is over . . . and we're both a little older." This is a direct reference of guidance and advice to me to wait to crack open the gates of heaven until the Iraq war is over and when he and I would be older, i.e. a combined age of seventy years old. He also sings in the same song, "Make a grave for the unknown soldier, nestled in your hollow shoulder." This has references to my prior military service and also my left shoulder injury that I described from the first volume of The New Wine.

My left shoulder often goes numb and feels "hollow." Also, it could have another double meaning that the gesture we make while saying the pledge of allegiance can often be an empty or "hollow" gesture. Yes, Jim and I both are incarnate and immortal sons of St. Mary, and we can see things many years in advance, and we can also go back in time and give new meaning to past events. This is the clear distinction between our two related kingdoms. One of them functions purely on linear time, the other is timeless and eternal, and both can influence the other.

For those The Doors music fans out there, let's take a look at some of Jim's lyrics and break them down some more. A favorite song of mine that I love singing is "Universal Mind."

Universal Mind

I was doing time in the universal mind

I was feeling fine

I was turning keys, I was setting people free

I was doing all right

Then you came along

With a suitcase and a song

Turned my head around

Now, I'm so alone

Just looking for a home

In every place I see

I'm the freedom man

I'm the freedom man

I'm the freedom man

That's how lucky I am

Let's take a close look at these lyrics and point to some things that should solidify my relationship with Jim. He refers to a "universal mind." This is a direct reference to what psychologist Carl Jung used to call "a universal consciousness." It's also how our other kingdom operates as well. The big mystery of the great beyond is this: imagine having immediate access in your mind to all the great thinkers in history that are living eternally in our other kingdom. Imagine feeling like every single day is a sunny day at the beach, regardless of what's going on in life. This is what it is like to be spiritually tethered to the other kingdom of heaven.

Yes, it is entirely possible to enter this state prior to death. In fact, once you do everything else in life takes on a different meaning. If you want to experience this feeling, I recommend doing three things. Number one, seek out your worst enemy and show them love. Number two, find a Catholic church and priest and receive holy sacraments. Number three, find a statue of St. Mary and ask her to show you at least one thing per day you can do for her or for someone else. If you do all these things with an open heart, welcome to our kingdom come.

In the song "Universal Mind," Jim references these "keys to the kingdom."

He says, "I was turning keys, I was setting people free, I was doing all right."

This is also a reference to his connection with his half brother and mother Mary and how we use the keys of "be love" and "believe" to ultimately set people free from sin and suffering and pain. Jim again references this as he calls himself "the freedom man." He is not being overly pretentious and is quite correct that that is his true spiritual identity given to him from birth. He goes on to sing "then you came along with a suitcase and a song, turned my head around." This is quite an interesting line, and to me, personally references my meeting my wife whose first name is "Carol," which is another word for a "song."

He talks of her "turning his head around" meaning the immediate attraction I felt for my future wife when I first met her.

He also sings, "That's how lucky I am." This is his exuberance of finding true love, and also, his love for his status being an immortal son of St. Mary that gets to set people free.

Let's closely examine another song written and performed by Jim Morrison with The Doors. The song is "Yes, the River Knows," and there are some very specific veiled references to the Jim to Matt reincarnation and relationship via St. Mary.

Yes, the River Knows

Please believe me

The river told me

Very softly

Want you to hold me, oooh

Free fall flow, river flow

On and on it goes

Breathe under water till the end

Free fall flow, river flow

On and on it goes

Breathe under water till the end

Yes, the river knows

Please believe me

If you don't need me

I'm going, but I need a little time

I promised I would drown myself in mystic heated wine

I'm going, but I need a little time

I promised I would drown myself in mystic heated wine

Free fall flow, river flow on and on it goes

Breathe under water until the end

Free fall flow, river flow

On and on it goes

Breathe under water until the end

With the lyrics of "please believe me, the river told me," Jim is focusing on the second of our keys of "believe" and how he's pleading for an audience that would include me in the future to "believe in him" and in who he is ultimately as a fraternal twin of St. Mary and his status of being conjoined with Matt in the present times.

The lines "I'm going, but I need a little time, I promised I would drown myself in mystic heated wine," refer once again to his knowledge of him "going" meaning leaving this world from his pending death in Paris in 1971, but he makes a promise to his audience of returning once again after a "little time" after he fulfills a promise to "drown himself in mystic heated wine."

This last line is extremely prophetic and the exact basis for both volumes I and II of The New Wine. Jim here, again references a drowning in "mystic" (sacramental or divine) heated wine (last name "Pinard" which is French for wine). The last few lines of "free fall flow, river flow, on and on it goes, breathe under water until the end" is more of instruction and encouragement to me in my life.

I have anxiety that I described as being related to trauma in my young life and Jim is saying, "Just go with the flow and try to breathe under water until the end."

He's recognizing my anxiety disorder which sometimes feels like trying to breathe under water, in spite of any immediate danger, but he knows the heavy burden I carry in my heart of trying to save a world that's teetering on it's very "end."

Let's take a look at Jim's lyrics to one of my favorite songs "The Crystal Ship," which, at first glance, appears to be written to an ex-girlfriend.

The Crystal Ship

Before you slip into unconsciousness

I'd like to have another kiss

Another flashing chance at bliss

Another kiss, another kiss

The days are bright and filled with pain

Enclose me in your gentle rain

The time you ran was too insane

We'll meet again, we'll meet again

Oh, tell me where your freedom lies

The streets are fields that never die

Deliver me from reasons why

You'd rather cry, I'd rather fly

The crystal ship is being filled

A thousand girls, a thousand thrills

A million ways to spend your time

When we get back, I'll drop a line

What Jim is describing here is not just the love he still felt for a former girlfriend; he is also describing the concept of "agape love" between God and man, and the "crystal ship" is a reference to a casket that we all travel in to the next life. He also makes mention of "freedom that lies in fields that never die," which is a description of the liberation we all gain in death as we are carried in our crystal ship into heaven which is like "fields that never die."

He's likening this trip to a great big gathering with a thousand girls and a thousand thrills, that death is ultimately nothing to fear, rather, it is like a grand celebration as you enter the other kingdom with its "giant family.

He describes death as merely "slipping into unconsciousness." It's a very interesting description here as I also recall that Paxton's family mentioned that before he "slipped into unconsciousness," he was only worried about the feelings of the wonderful family that he was leaving behind.

Let's now look at another very popular The Doors song entitled "The Soft Parade." The lyrics of this song are highly prophetic and also show many instances of the Jim to Matt reincarnation theory.

The Soft Parade

When I was back there in seminary school

There was a person there

Who put forth the proposition

That you can petition the Lord with prayer

Petition the Lord with prayer

Petition the Lord with prayer

You cannot petition the Lord with prayer!

Can you give me sanctuary

I must find a place to hide

A place for me to hide

Can you find me soft asylum

I can't make it anymore

The man is at the door

Peppermint, miniskirts, chocolate candy

Champion sax and a girl named Sandy

There's only four ways to get unraveled

One is to sleep and the other is travel, da, da

One is a bandit up in the hills

One is to love your neighbor till

His wife gets home

Catacombs

Nursery bones

Winter women

Growing stones

Carrying babies

To the river

Streets and shoes

Avenues

Leather riders

Selling news

The monk bought lunch

Ha, ha, he bought a little

Yes, he did

Woo!

This is the best part of the trip

This is the trip, the best part

I really like what'd he say?

Yeah!

Yeah, right!

Pretty good, huh

Huh!

Yeah, I'm proud to be a part of this number

Successful hills are here to stay

Everything must be this way

Gentle streets where people play

Welcome to the soft parade

All our lives we sweat and save

Building for a shallow grave

Must be something else we say

Somehow to defend this place

Everything must be this way

Everything must be this way, yeah

The soft parade has now begun

Listen to the engines hum

People out to have some fun

A cobra on my left

Leopard on my right, yeah

The deer woman in a silk dress

Girls with beads around their necks

Kiss the hunter of the green vest

98 99

Who has wrestled before

With lions in the night

Out of sight!

The lights are getting brighter

The radio is moaning

Calling to the dogs

There are still a few animals

Left out in the yard

But it's getting harder

To describe sailors

To the underfed

Tropic corridor

Tropic treasure

What got us this far

To this mild equator?

We need someone or something new

Something else to get us through, yeah, c'mon

Callin' on the dogs

Callin' on the dog

Oh, it's gettin' harder

Callin' on the dogs

Callin' in the dogs

Callin' all the dogs

Callin' on the gods

You gotta meet me

Too late, baby

Slay a few animals

At the crossroads

Too late

All in the yard

But it's gettin' harder

By the crossroads

You gotta meet me

Oh, we're goin', we're goin' great

At the edge of town

Tropic corridor

Tropic treasure

Havin' a good time

Got to come along

What got us this far

To this mild equator?

Outskirts of the city

You and I

We need someone new

Somethin' new

Somethin' else to get us through

Better bring your gun

Better bring your gun

Tropic corridor

Tropic treasure

We're gonna ride and have some fun

When all else fails

We can whip the horse's eyes

And make them sleep

And cry

This is one of the more talked about The Doors songs as it was written and performed near the end of Jim's life, and you can see most of it is veiled religious references. He talks of "petitioning the Lord with prayer" and that you "can't petition the Lord with prayer." This is his pleading with me, who was with him in spirit to help him in his life. Jim had just recently been wrongfully convicted of indecent exposure and sentenced to six months in prison for a crime that not one person at the Miami concert in 1969 saw him commit.

He, soon after, moved to Paris in 1971 to become a poet and was very depressed by the fact he could not walk the streets of Paris freely because of his immense fame as a rock singer. Thus, he talks of needing a "sanctuary" or "place to hide" and the "man is at the door." "The man" in the 1960s was another word for cops or police. This line also has relevance in my own life now with Jim as I was recently called and threatened over the phone by a police detective who I later found out was being sued in civil court for illegal search and seizures with the most absurd stalking charges ever. This detective got himself in a lot of hot water once I called his supervisor to let him know what he was up to.

This event was also highlighted in the poem "An American Prayer" which predicted a "loose obedience to a vegetable law" as preceding the return of the Christian kingdom. In this song, Jim also sings about "kiss the hunter of the green vest who has wrestled before with lions in the night." This is a direct plea for the world to embrace me as a son of St. Mary. In the army, we wore green "vests" as part of our class A uniforms. He's saying that I am a hunter of lions in the night which are Lucifer or Satan/Hillel and all his demonic spirits that are on his "branch of the night."

Jim also sings here of "the lights are getting brighter," and the "radio is moaning," and also "it's getting harder to describe sailors to the underfed." These descriptions are of the "quickening" that I felt as I cracked open the gates of heaven in the fall of 2016, and how then once fully conjoined with my half brother James who I literally raised from the dead that all our physical and spiritual senses were heightened in our body. Lights looked brighter, the radio started sounding better. He describes how it's difficult to describe such spiritual phenomena to those who are spiritually underfed and have never experienced a transfiguring event such as I did in the fall of 2016. Jim also speaks of "slaying animals at the crossroads."

This is a deliberate religious reference to sacrificing animals to "please God" and how when we started running in the night with the devil or Lucifer that he would meet us at "the crossroads" of life where the devil is said to be in waiting for all of us during crucial crossroads of our lives. Jim also sings, "When all else fails, we can whip the horses' eyes and make them scream and cry." Here, he is pleading with me of how to handle "the horses" which are the seven orbiting planets of Nibiru as described earlier and trying to prevent them from disrupting life on planet earth by "whipping their eyes to make them sleep and cry." He's saying we still can try to do something to save mankind by changing the trajectory of these planets orbiting the second sun that is passing by earth as destructive judgment of God and how he and I can try to change the outcome and alter their orbital paths through prayer.

Let's look at another of one of my favorite Doors songs entitled "L.A. Woman."

L.A. Woman

Well, I just got into town about an hour ago

Took a look around, see which way the wind blow

Where the little girls in their Hollywood bungalows?

Are you a lucky little lady in the city of light?

Or just another lost angel

City of night

City of night

City of night

City of night

Woo, c'mon

102 103

L.A. woman

L.A. woman

L.A. woman, Sunday afternoon

L.A. woman, Sunday afternoon

L.A. woman, Sunday afternoon

Drive through your suburbs

Into your blues

Into your blues, yeah

Into your blue, blue, blues

Into your blues

Ohh, yeah

I see your hair is burnin'

Hills are filled with fire

If they say I never loved you

You know they are a liar

Drivin' down your freeways

Midnight alleys roam

Cops in cars, the topless bars

Never saw a woman

So alone, so alone

So alone, so alone

Motel money, murder madness

Let's change the mood from glad to sadness

Mr. Mojo risin', Mr. Mojo risin'

Mr. Mojo risin', Mr. Mojo risin'

Got to keep on risin'

Mr. Mojo risin', Mr. Mojo risin'

Mojo risin', gotta Mojo risin'

Mr. Mojo risin', gotta keep on risin'

Ridin', ridin'

Gone ridin', ridin'

Gone ridin', ridin'

I gotta ridin', ridin'

Well, ridin', ridin'

I gotta, wooo, yeah, ridin'

Woah

Yeah

Well, I just got into town about an hour ago

Took a look around, see which way the wind blow

Where the little girls in their Hollywood bungalows?

Are you a lucky little lady in the city of light?

Or just another lost angel

City of night

City of night

City of night

City of night

Woah, c'mon

L.A. woman

L.A. woman

L.A. woman, you're my woman

Oh little L.A. woman, little L.A. woman

L.A. Woman, woman

L.A. woman, c'mon

This is one of the more popular and often played Doors songs. What's interesting is in college, I dated and fell in love with an L.A. woman from California. I foolishly believed it was true love but found out I was simply being used to enact revenge on an ex-boyfriend. The relationship didn't last more than a summer and led me "into my blues."

The song also talks of "angels in a city of night," and this refers to all of us as "angels" in a world that is still fallen and "in the night."

The song also references the anagram for Jim Morrison being "Mojo Risin'" and how after he and I cracked open the gates of heaven in the fall of 2016, he would be "fully risen" as a son of St. Mary and that he needs to "keep on risin'" with me to fulfill the rest of our mission to "save our city."

This reference of saving "the city" is also described on another favorite song of mine "Roadhouse Blues" where Jim sings about St. Mary with the lyrics of "ashen lady, ashen lady, give up your vows, give up your vows, save our city, save our city, right now."

The "ashen lady" that Jim speaks of is St. Mary. In fact, I will post another photo of the statue of St. Mary from my local church at St. Mary's in Spring Lake, Michigan. The statue which Jim described as an "idol with hollow eyes" is also the "ashen lady" because the complexion of her skin appears "ashen."

I want to take a closer look at one last The Doors song for the time being. The song is "The End," and it is my all-time favorite of Jim's songs. It is fitting for today's world which is near end times.

The End

This is the end, beautiful friend

This is the end, my only friend, the end

Of our elaborate plans, the end

Of everything that stands, the end

No safety or surprise, the end

I'll never look into your eyes, again

Can you picture what will be, so limitless and free

Desperately in need, of some, stranger's hand

In a, desperate land

Lost in a Roman wilderness of pain

And all the children are insane, all the children are insane

Waiting for the summer rain, yeah

There's danger on the edge of town

Ride the king's highway, baby

Weird scenes inside the gold mine

Ride the highway west, baby

Ride the snake, ride the snake

To the lake, the ancient lake, baby

The snake is long, seven miles

Ride the snake, he's old, and his skin is cold

The west is the best, the west is the best

Get here, and we'll do the rest

The blue bus is callin' us, the blue bus is callin' us

Driver, where you takin' us

The killer awoke before dawn, he put his boots on

He took a face from the ancient gallery

And he walked on down the hall

He went into the room where his sister lived, and, then he

Paid a visit to his brother, and then he

He walked on down the hall, and

And he came to a door, and he looked inside

Father, yes son, I want to kill you

Mother, I want to, fuck you

C'mon baby, take a chance with us

C'mon baby, take a chance with us

C'mon baby, take a chance with us

And meet me at the back of the blue bus

Doin' a blue rock, on a blue bus

Doin' a blue rock, c'mon, yeah

Kill, kill, kill, kill, kill, kill

This is the end, beautiful friend

This is the end, my only friend, the end

It hurts to set you free

But you'll never follow me

The end of laughter and soft lies

The end of nights we tried to die

This is the end

This amazing song was often a fan favorite at concerts. It also has many, many veiled references to the Jim to Matt conjoining and reincarnation. First, he describes "the end" by saying "this is the end of our elaborate plans, the end." The "elaborate plans" he is referring to is the mission that was originally designed by St. Mary for her incarnate sons being James Douglas Morrison and Matthew Douglas Pinard, and how Jim recording his music would later serve as prophecies and time markers to Matt to come in and pick up after. He also sings of "the blue bus is calling us" which again is a reference to my own military service and how "we" being myself with Jim were driven around on blue buses throughout training. He also sings of "desperately in need of some stranger's hand in a desperate land."

This is highly prophetic of our current times. We all are force to live in a "desperate" land due to the constant threat of nuclear war and also that we are all trapped in a "Roman wilderness of pain" in that this world is fueled by idolatry and greed. With the line "can you picture what will be, so limitless and free," is his encouragement to me that no matter how this all turns out, I will gain entry back into the other kingdom. He reaffirms this with the lines, "it hurts to set you free, but you'll never follow me." This is also encouragement to me that no matter what happens, we did our job of trying to warn and change mankind, but since no one listened, they will not follow us into heaven. He is also saying that since this world is at such odds with the Holy Trinity that a "stranger's hand" in greeting Jim and I today, will feel more comfortable than the friends and family that will deny us and alienate us out of fear.

Jim also refers again to "the snake is long, seven miles, he's old, and his skin is cold" and that this is near "an ancient lake." Again, as I first introduced in the first volume of The New Wine, this refers to Jim and I being conjoined at age seventy years old and the circulation problems I sometimes have in my feet and that I live near Lake Michigan which is an ancient lake. The children being insane is the reference to all humans who are victims of Lucifer or Hillel's constant agitation of them and that they are all "waiting for the summer rain," which is a reference to when I would finally publish the first volume of The New Wine in the summer of 2017. He describes again foreseeing the violent murder on my army base with the prophetic lines, "The killer awoke before dawn, he put his boots on." Then, he is pleading for the world to "come on, baby, take a chance with us and meet me at the back of the blue bus, on a blue rock." The blue rock is an interesting line and seemingly has no meaning. However, look closely at my high school football photo below and, in particular, pay attention to the blue jersey I am wearing and what it says.

Photo: Pay close attention to my high school football jersey here. Jim sings on "The End" to "take a chance with us and meet us on the back of the blue bus, on a blue rock." My jersey is blue and says "Shamrocks" on it. I am Jim's "blue rock" he prophesied about on the song "The End." I always found it quite amusing that the best quarterback on our Catholic High School was actually Jesus himself who was benched for having a "poor attitude" and "leadership problem."

Photo: This is Jim's "ashen lady" with "hollow idol eyes" that he sings of with The Doors found in St. Mary's Catholic Church in Spring Lake, Michigan. James and Matthew are St. Mary's fraternal twin sons. She is holding her arms open as an invitation to the entire world to join us on our new vine with our new wine.

Photo: A closer view of Jim's "Pirate Prince" at her side that Jim sang of on the song "Wild Child" near the altar at St. Mary's Catholic Church in Spring Lake, Michigan. He appears like a "pirate" because of the blood dripping from the cross. This is the first son, Jesus Christ, who is actually St. Mary's "Prince of Peace."

Photo: This is the altar at another local church St. Rose Catholic Church in Hastings, Michigan. I often pray here and find it to be a very powerful place as well. Notice the words, "Sanctus, Sanctus, Sanctus" written on the ceiling above Jesus Christ. In the 1991 The Doors movie, Val Kilmer playing Jim Morrison stated, "the people want something sacred." Sanctus is the singular for "sacred" or "sacramental." Now, when I pray I recite "Sancti, Sancti, Sancti." I don't know why I started doing this, however,

"Sancti" is the plural for "Sanctus." I believe I do this because of the spiritual fusing that took place among St. Mary's sons in the fall of 2016, and the sons of St. Mary are now conjoined as "Sancti Sons."

Photo: The hanging body of Jesus Christ in St. Rose Catholic Church in Hastings, Michigan, showing his crucifixion. Notice the spear wound once again shown incorrectly on his right side. Jesus was pierced with a Roman spear on his left side which is the side I have an interesting unexplainable birthmark a top my left rib cage.

Photo: The first son Jesus Christ walking among "lambs" inside St. Rose Catholic Church in Hastings, Michigan. Jesus is the "Lamb of God" or "sacrificial lamb."

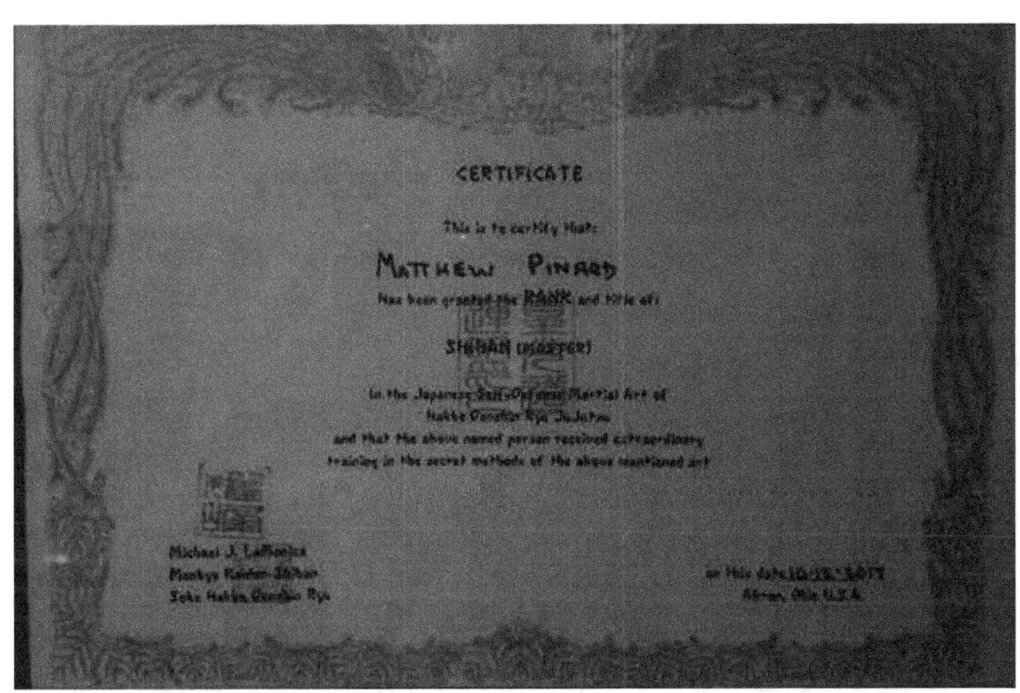

Photo: The above certificate was awarded to me this past fall of 2017 granting me the rank of Shihan (Master) or 6th Dan in ancient samurai genji battlefield Japanese style Jujutsu after twelve years of intense and focused training under Soke Michael LaMonica of the Eighth Light Dojo in Akron, Ohio.

After over a decade of very rigorous and technically demanding training, I was recently awarded the rank of Shihan (Master) or 6th Degree Dan/Black Belt in an ancient samurai battlefield Japanese style of Jujutsu. The ryu or "school" I am a part of is called "Hakko Denshin Ryu Jujutsu" which literally translates to "Eighth Light Art School." Our moan for our school features a set of purple rectangles that symbolize the eighth light which is the color purple signifying royalty in Japan.

The founder of this incredibly powerful martial art was a man named Okayama Ryuho who philosophically conceived that there are nine color bands in the sun's color spectrum. The eighth of these nine bands, which he referred to as a shade of red or purple, holds the secret of the power of Hakko-ryu Jujutsu. This eighth light of which the founder spoke of seems at first very "weak" in composition; but, in fact, it is surprisingly powerful.

The art goes on to explain that the ninth band—the color purple—creates and develops the eighth light. Purple is also the color of royalty and honor in Japan. A photo below shows me training in this art as our school's purple banner can be seen in the background.

Photo: Matthew Douglas Pinard a ranked Shihan (Master) or 6th degree Dan throwing a would-be attacker using principles found in the art of Japanese Hakko denshin Ryu Jujutsu.

The reason I am discussing this amazingly powerful martial art that I have studied for over a decade is because of the spiritual principles that are found within it. This martial art was at one time the official "humane" martial art taught to both police and military in Japan in the 1940s. It specifically focuses on techniques that require tremendous focus and uses counterintuitive principles such as relaxation and proper body structure to easily defeat an opponent twice your size who may be seemingly much stronger.

The founder once likened our techniques to water being primed in a pump, if properly focused, water that is primed and under pressure can cause tremendous force as we can sometimes see it do the same in nature. I, personally, was put into atrial fibrillation by my instructor just with proper technique applied to my wrist. I also caused a fellow student to lose all bowel function with a properly applied technique to the wrist.

We focus in Hakko Denshin Ryu on the meridian lines within the body that we can attack to disrupt internal organ function as well as cause excruciating pain to convince a would-be attacker to discontinue his attack. It is a humane art that does not resort to violence or to trying to deliberately harm or cause injury. That being said, we can inflict a tremendous amount of pain in the body without leaving permanent damage. I believe there are incredible principles in this art that carry over to life. Sometimes, we have been deliberately harmed by others either physically or emotionally and we wish to seek revenge to try to destroy them.

This art focuses on using humane techniques to change aggressive behaviors of others. It also teaches us to remain calm and actually relaxed within our body as an offensive attack is occurring. This has tremendous spiritual relevance. Often times, life comes at us and hands us things that are tragic and unexpected, and we sometimes get angry at God or lose our faith. This art would teach to remain calm, trust in the purpose behind what may be happening and be relaxed even in the midst of the storm.

This past mid-January 2018, my wife and I were gone over Christmas for two days to visit relatives on the east side of Detroit. While we were gone, we had a break-in at our home. The police were called and found large footprints across the front of our yard. We also noticed that nothing "valuable" was taken from our home. What was taken was my Christian cross, the one that bent in half after Paxton's death. This was clearly a message of intimidation. A few nights later, my mother St. Mary, replied with her response.

A meteor flew across the sky in southern Michigan and broke up into pieces and caused a 2.0 earthquake near Detroit. Many residents heard the boom and felt the ground shake. St. Mary is delivering a clear message as well. Future attempts to intimidate, harass, or threaten her risen sons will be met with destruction on a level that far super cedes what any man can enact here on earth. This is not meant to frighten or scare anyone except those responsible for the breaking and entering at my home. What I am trying to impart upon these types of individuals is responses like that one below will only grow in intensity and scope whether or not St. Mary's Son is killed, abducted, harassed, or detained/incarcerated illegally. I would take this quite seriously.

Photo: A six-foot wide meteor screams across Michigan skies in mid-January 2018 as St. Mary's response to those parties who illegally broke into her son's home in an attempt to threaten and intimidate the release of *The New Wine* series of books.

I would like to now leave us all with a few final thoughts. As I sit and think about how I want to end the second volume of The New Wine, I can't help but reflect on the tremendous life and inspiration and example set by my young friend and fraternal twin Paxton Elkins. I only knew him for a little over a year, but the courage and light that this child was is unlike any I've ever seen.

His family told me as his body was failing and he was moving on to a bigger and better purpose in the other kingdom, he only cared about the feelings of those around him. He was comforting all of us as he lay dying of a disease that is insidious and should have been cured decades ago. I remember telling his family that his short life could possibly bring world peace through showing the world that there is another dimension among us that will simply not allow for there to be a third globally devastating world war.

This is the amazing image I ponder as I recall the vision St. Mary gave me the morning of his funeral of the thousands of white-winged doves falling from the sky and turning into lit candles that landed on the white stone crosses of the fallen soldiers in Arlington National Cemetery. I wish to end this second volume of The New Wine with two original poems written by both Jim and I called "Peace Town" and "Purple and Free." "Peace Town" is in honor of young Paxton Elkins whose name translates to the same.

"Purple and Free" is in honor of the African-American man I met on the street of Grand Rapids, Michigan, who was asking for monetary donations as he sat helplessly in his "steel prison;" a wheelchair. I pray that the sacrifice of Paxton's life and the man I called "St. Charles" brings total peace to a world that is at present in complete opposition to the will of its maker. May God's peace be with us all.

Peace Town

In memoriam of Paxton Nathaniel Elkins

You broke the bonds of this world and left us on a Sunday morn'
A lifeless body flew off the cross of Calvary's hill into the sky
A white-winged dove carried you up, up, up to new found castles on high
Your family and friends did cry, sigh, and now forever mourn

An army of white-winged doves fell down from your wings above
They carried your light, a myriad of lit candles, signs of your agape love
As they fell one by one onto the white stone crosses in the ground
Soldiers they were, now forever alive,
eternally reborn to thrive in our time

Your name means "peace town" and this day we reflect and pray
That the world wakes up and sees the debt you have paid
There shall not be even one more death or blood shed now forever more
Not one more soldier in Paxton's Army will be left stranded on the shore

Rank and file, they now approach onto beaches now stormed
By ancient souls seeking the revenge of their untimely demise
Pounding the drum of peace, not war, screamin' across unending shores
Of countless beaches and tides that pull
forth souls as numerous as the sands

Of time we now ponder and seek to end a

ll wars eternally, depart now death

We speak now of an end to war, we shall fight

no more, no senseless blood shed

That settles no score among men, we of sun dome

now in the dark of night

Hold your life above all others to be extolled, forever bathed in her light

Matthew Douglas Pinard and James Douglas Morrison

Purple and Free

Dedicated to "St. Charles"

I shook his trembling hand and watched his unbound knees sway
in the breeze Saint Charles was he, bound by his
chair, a cold steel prison for he
For I had not the heart to tell him, I now know why
Maya's caged bird does sing
I couldn't wait to tell him there was a new Sun Queen, Oprah Win Free.

The color of purple is she, her heart shaped sun over Chicago now seen
to declare her chosen people from the continent shaped like our minds
African drums beating like the hearts of native peoples seeking to find
our mother's veiled face in the new sun, above a toll booth collecting.

A fee for her children who pass through headed west
on a highway now free
this other kingdom is now by far the best, my
old friend Martin Luther King
Did he not see that mountaintop sitting just out of
reach for you and for me
for he and I and Oprah, Ellen, and Portia have
one dream, a shout and scream.

Free at last, free at last, thank God almighty we are free at last

For Bono's colors now bleed, into Van's mystic we now all float downstream
This win's for Ray, Robby, John and Me, open our Doors now eternally
Her son's rays shoot down from her veil and sleeves,
Mary and me, help us all

To see, that we are all his children, all
colors, genders, our flock is now free
The toll has been paid, by her scattered
sons, three nails and a crown of three
For Stevie's white-winged dove was but in the
nicks of time, a bell tower did
Chime calling back the shepherd to his sheep, opening
up the leper's eyes to see
Her immortal Sun Kings and Queens

Matthew Douglas Pinard and James Douglas Morrison

About the Author

Matthew Douglas Pinard is the author of The New Wine series. He was born and raised in southeastern Michigan and has a bachelor's degree in psychology from the University of Michigan and a master's degree in military history from Louisiana State University. Matthew is also a former US Army JAG legal specialist. He and his wife Carol Rose are recent transplants from west Michigan and now live in beautiful Prescott Valley, Arizona, with their two dogs Reese, a chocolate Lab, and Cleetus, a Redbone Coonhound. Matthew is a ranked Shihan (sixth degree) in Hakko Den shin Ryu Japanese Jujutsu and enjoys hiking, communing with the other side, praying for world peace, and photographing archangels in his spare time.

Other Books by Author Matthew

matthewpinardauthor.com

Follow Me:

- [Goodreads](#)
- [Author Central](#)
- [YouTube](#)

Screenplay Awards Matthew Douglas Pinard

Official Selection

    Bloodstained Indie Film Festival

    StoryPros Awards Screenplay Contest

    Military Script Showcase

    L.A. Neo Noir Novel Film & Script Festival

    True Story International Film Festival

    Reel Heart International Film Festival

    Hollywood Boulevard International Film Festival

    Independent Talents International Film Festival

    Fort Worth Indie Film Showcase

    California Independent Film Festival

    San Pedro International Film Festival,

    Southeastern International Film Festival

    Louisiana International Film Festival

    Official Selection

First Ten Pages Script Contest

Atlanta Comedy Film Festival

Georgia Shorts Film Festival

Official Finalist

Las Vegas International Film and Screenwriting Contest, Honorable Mention

Depth of Field International Film Festival, Award Winner

Beverly Hills International Film Festival, Silver Winner

Queen Palm International Film Festival, Award Winner

Colorado International Film Festival, Quarter-Finalist

Chicago Screenplay Awards, Quarter-Finalist

NYC International Screenplay Awards, Quarter-Finalist

Atlanta Screenplay Awards, Semi-Finalist

Cordillera International Film Festival, Semi-Finalist

Fade In Awards, Finalist

Breaking Walls Thriller Screenplay Award Winner

Vegas Movie Awards,

The Santa Barbara International Screenplay Awards, Finalist

Miami Screen Play Awards, Quarter-Finalist:

www.ingramcontent.com/pod-product-compliance
Lightning Source LLC
Chambersburg PA
CBHW081359070526
44583CB00020B/2599